The Sublime and Beautiful

The Sublime and Beautiful

Edmund Burke

MINT EDITIONS

This book was originally published as: *A Philosophical Inquiry into the Origin of Our Ideas of The Sublime and Beautiful* in 1757.

This edition published by Mint Editions 2020.

ISBN 9781513268774 | E-ISBN 9781513273778

Published by Mint Editions®

 MINT
EDITIONS

minteditionbooks.com

Publishing Director: Jennifer Newens
Design & Production: Rachel Lopez Metzger
Typesetting: Westchester Publishing Services

Contents

Part 4

PART 1

Section 1

Novelty

The first and the simplest emotion which we discover in the human mind is curiosity. By curiosity I mean whatever desire we have for, or whatever pleasure we take in, novelty. We see children perpetually running from place to place, to hunt out something new: they catch with great eagerness, and with very little choice, at whatever comes before them; their attention is engaged by everything, because everything has, in that stage of life, the charm of novelty to recommend it. But as those things, which engage us merely by their novelty, cannot attach us for any length of time, curiosity is the most superficial of all the affections; it changes its object perpetually; it has an appetite which is very sharp, but very easily satisfied; and it has always an appearance of giddiness, restlessness, and anxiety. Curiosity, from its nature, is a very active principle; it quickly runs over the greatest part of its objects, and soon exhausts the variety which is commonly to be met with in nature; the same things make frequent returns, and they return with less and less of any agreeable effect. In short, the occurrences of life, by the time we come to know it a little, would be incapable of affecting the mind with any other sensations than those of loathing and weariness, if many things were not adapted to affect the mind by means of other powers besides novelty in them, and of other passions besides curiosity in ourselves. These powers and passions shall be considered in their place. But, whatever these powers are, or upon what principle soever they affect the mind, it is absolutely necessary that they should not be exerted in those things which a daily and vulgar use have brought into a stale unaffecting familiarity. Some degree of novelty must be one of the materials in every instrument which works upon the mind; and curiosity blends itself more or less with all our passions.

Section 2

Pain and Pleasure

It seems, then, necessary towards moving the passions of people advanced in life to any considerable degree, that the objects designed for that purpose, besides their being in some measure new, should be capable of exciting pain or pleasure from other causes. Pain and pleasure are simple ideas, incapable of definition. People are not liable to be mistaken in their feelings, but they are very frequently wrong in the names they give them, and in their reasonings about them. Many are of opinion, that pain arises necessarily from the removal of some pleasure; as they think pleasure does from the ceasing or diminution of some pain. For my part, I am rather inclined to imagine, that pain and pleasure, in their most simple and natural manner of affecting, are each of a positive nature, and by no means necessarily dependent on each other for their existence. The human mind is often, and I think it is for the most part, in a state neither of pain nor pleasure, which I call a state of indifference. When I am carried from this state into a state of actual pleasure, it does not appear necessary that I should pass through the medium of any sort of pain. If in such a state of indifference, or ease, or tranquillity, or call it what you please, you were to be suddenly entertained with a concert of music; or suppose some object of a fine shape, and bright, lively colors, to be presented before you; or imagine your smell is gratified with the fragrance of a rose; or if, without any previous thirst, you were to drink of some pleasant kind of wine, or to taste of some sweetmeat without being hungry; in all the several senses, of hearing, smelling, and tasting, you undoubtedly find a pleasure; yet, if I inquire into the state of your mind previous to these gratifications, you will hardly tell me that they found you in any kind of pain; or, having satisfied these several senses with their several pleasures, will you say that any pain has succeeded, though the pleasure is absolutely over? Suppose, on the other hand, a man in the same state of indifference to receive a violent blow, or to drink of some bitter potion, or to have his ears wounded with some harsh and grating sound; here is no removal of pleasure; and yet here is felt, his every sense which is affected, a pain very distinguishable. It may be said, perhaps, that the pain in these cases had its rise from the removal of the pleasure which the man enjoyed before, though that pleasure was of so low a degree as to be perceived only by the removal. But this seems to me a subtilty that is not discoverable in nature. For if, previous to the pain, I do not feel any actual pleasure, I have no reason to judge that any such thing exists; since pleasure is only pleasure as it is felt. The same may be said of pain, and with equal reason. I can never persuade myself that pleasure and pain are mere relations, which can only exist as they are contrasted; but I think I can discern clearly that there are positive pains and pleasures, which do not at all depend upon each other. Nothing is more certain to my own feelings than this. There is nothing which I can distinguish in my mind with more clearness than the three states, of indifference, of pleasure, and of pain. Every one of these I can perceive without any sort of idea of its relation to anything else. Caius is afflicted with a fit of the colic; this man is actually in pain; stretch Caius upon the rack, he will feel a much greater pain: but does this pain of the rack arise from the removal of any pleasure? or is the fit of the colic a pleasure or a pain just as we are pleased to consider it?

Section 3

THE DIFFERENCE BETWEEN THE REMOVAL OF PAIN AND POSITIVE PLEASURE

We shall carry this proposition yet a step further. We shall venture to propose, that pain and pleasure are not only not necessarily dependent for their existence on their mutual diminution or removal, but that, in reality, the diminution or ceasing of pleasure does not operate like positive pain; and that the removal or diminution of pain, in its effect, has very little resemblance to positive pleasure.[1] The former of these propositions will, I believe, be much more readily allowed than the latter; because it is very evident that pleasure, when it has run its career, sets us down very nearly where it found us. Pleasure of every kind quickly satisfies; and, when it is over, we relapse into indifference, or, rather, we fall into a soft tranquillity which is tinged with the agreeable color of the former sensation. I own it is not at first view so apparent that the removal of a great pain does not resemble positive pleasure: but let us recollect in what state we have found our minds upon escaping some imminent danger, or on being released from the severity of some cruel pain. We have on such occasions found, if I am not much mistaken, the temper of our minds in a tenor very remote from that which attends the presence of positive pleasure; we have found them in a state of much sobriety, impressed with a sense of awe, in a sort of tranquillity shadowed with horror. The fashion of the countenance and the gesture of the body on such occasions is so correspondent to this state of mind, that any person, a stranger to the cause of the appearance, would rather judge us under some consternation, than in the enjoyment of anything like positive pleasure.

> *"As when a wretch, who, conscious of his crime,*
> *Pursued for murder from his native clime,*

---

1. Mr. Locke [Essay on Human Understanding, l. ii. c. 20, sect. 16,] thinks that the removal or lessening of a pain is considered and operates as a pleasure, and the loss or diminishing of pleasure as a pain. It is this opinion which we consider here.

Just gains some frontier, breathless, pale, amazed;
All gaze, all wonder!"

—Illiad

This striking appearance of the man whom Homer supposes to have just escaped an imminent danger, the sort of mixed passion of terror and surprise, with which he affects the spectators, paints very strongly the manner in which we find ourselves affected upon occasions any way similar. For when we have suffered from any violent emotion, the mind naturally continues in something like the same condition, after the cause which first produced it has ceased to operate. The tossing of the sea remains after the storm; and when this remain of horror has entirely subsided, all the passion which the accident raised subsides along with it; and the mind returns to its usual state of indifference. In short, pleasure (I mean anything either in the inward sensation, or in the outward appearance, like pleasure from a positive cause) has never, I imagine, its origin from the removal of pain or danger.

Section 4

OF DELIGHT AND PLEASURE, AS OPPOSED TO EACH OTHER

But shall we therefore say, that the removal of pain or its diminution is always simply painful? or affirm that the cessation or the lessening of pleasure is always attended itself with a pleasure? By no means. What I advance is no more than this; first, that there are pleasures and pains of a positive and independent nature; and, secondly, that the feeling which results from the ceasing or diminution of pain does not bear a sufficient resemblance to positive pleasure, to have it considered as of the same nature, or to entitle it to be known by the same name; and thirdly, that upon the same principle the removal or qualification of pleasure has no resemblance to positive pain. It is certain that the former feeling (the removal or moderation of pain) has something in it far from distressing, or disagreeable in its nature. This feeling, in many cases so agreeable, but in all so different from positive pleasure, has no name which I know; but that hinders not its being a very real one, and very different from all others. It is most certain, that every species of satisfaction or pleasure, how different soever in its manner of affecting, is of a positive nature in the mind of him who feels it. The affection is undoubtedly positive; but the cause may be, as in this case it certainly is, a sort of *privation*. And it is very reasonable that we should distinguish by some term two things so distinct in nature, as a pleasure that is such simply, and without any relation, from that pleasure which cannot exist without a relation, and that, too, a relation to pain. Very extraordinary it would be, if these affections, so distinguishable in their causes, so different in their effects, should be confounded with each other, because vulgar use has ranged them under the same general title. Whenever I have occasion to speak of this species of relative pleasure, I call it *delight*; and I shall take the best care I can to use that word in no other sense. I am satisfied the word is not commonly used in this appropriated signification; but I thought it better to take up a word already known, and to limit its signification, than to introduce a new one, which would not perhaps incorporate so well with the language. I should never have presumed the least alteration in our words, if the nature of the language, framed for the purposes of business rather than those of philosophy, and the nature of my subject, that leads me out of the common track of discourse, did not in a manner necessitate me to it. I shall make use of this liberty with all possible caution. As I make use of the word *delight* to express the sensation which accompanies the removal of pain or danger, so, when I speak of positive pleasure, I shall for the most part call it simply *pleasure*.

Section 5

JOY AND GRIEF

It must be observed, that the cessation of pleasure affects the mind three ways. If it simply ceases after having continued a proper time, the effect is *indifference*; if it be abruptly broken off, there ensues an uneasy sense called *disappointment*; if the object be so totally lost that there is no chance of enjoying it again, a passion arises in the mind which is called *grief*. Now there is none of these, not even grief, which is the most violent, that I think has any resemblance to positive pain. The person who grieves suffers his passion to grow upon him; he indulges it, he loves it: but this never happens in the case of actual pain, which no man ever willingly endured for any considerable time. That grief should be willingly endured, though far from a simply pleasing sensation, is not so difficult to be understood. It is the nature of grief to keep its object perpetually in its eye, to present it in its most pleasurable views, to repeat all the circumstances that attend it, even to the last minuteness; to go back to every particular enjoyment, to dwell upon each, and to find a thousand new perfections in all, that were not sufficiently understood before; in grief, the *pleasure* is still uppermost; and the affliction we suffer has no resemblance to absolute pain, which is always odious, and which we endeavor to shake off as soon as possible. The Odyssey of Homer, which abounds with so many natural and affecting images, has none more striking than those which Menelaus raises of the calamitous fate of his friends, and his own manner of feeling it. He owns, indeed, that he often gives himself some intermission from such melancholy reflections; but he observes, too, that, melancholy as they are, they give him pleasure.

> "*Still in short intervals of* pleasing woe,
> *Regardful of the friendly dues I owe,*
> *I to the glorious dead, forever dear,*
> Indulge *the tribute of a* grateful *tear.*"
>
> —Hom. Od.

EDMUND BURKE

On the other hand, when we recover our health, when we escape an imminent danger, is it with joy that we are affected? The sense on these occasions is far from that smooth and voluptuous satisfaction which the assured prospect of pleasure bestows. The delight which arises from the modifications of pain confesses the stock from whence it sprung, in its solid, strong, and severe nature.

Section 6

OF THE PASSIONS WHICH BELONG TO SELF-PRESERVATION

Most of the ideas which are capable of making a powerful impression on the mind, whether simply of pain or pleasure, or of the modifications of those, may be reduced very nearly to these two heads, *self-preservation*, and *society*; to the ends of one or the other of which all our passions are calculated to answer. The passions which concern self-preservation, turn mostly on *pain* or *danger*. The ideas of *pain*, *sickness*, and *death*, fill the mind with strong emotions of horror; but *life* and *health*, though they put us in a capacity of being affected with pleasure, make no such impression by the simple enjoyment. The passions therefore which are conversant about the preservation of the individual turn chiefly on *pain* and *danger*, and they are the most powerful of all the passions.

Section 7

OF THE SUBLIME

Whatever is fitted in any sort to excite the ideas of pain and danger, that is to say, whatever is in any sort terrible, or is conversant about terrible objects, or operates in a manner analogous to terror, is a source of the *sublime*; that is, it is productive of the strongest emotion which the mind is capable of feeling. I say the strongest emotion, because I am satisfied the ideas of pain are much more powerful than those which enter on the part of pleasure. Without all doubt, the torments which we may be made to suffer are much greater in their effect on the body and mind, than any pleasures which the most learned voluptuary could suggest, or than the liveliest imagination, and the most sound and exquisitely sensible body, could enjoy. Nay, I am in great doubt whether any man could be found, who would earn a life of the most perfect satisfaction at the price of ending it in the torments, which justice inflicted in a few hours on the late unfortunate regicide in France. But as pain is stronger in its operation than pleasure, so death is in general a much more affecting idea than pain; because there are very few pains, however exquisite, which are not preferred to death: nay, what generally makes pain itself, if I may say so, more painful, is, that it is considered as an emissary of this king of terrors. When danger or pain press too nearly, they are incapable of giving any delight, and are simply terrible; but at certain distances, and with certain modifications, they may be, and they are, delightful, as we every day experience. The cause of this I shall endeavor to investigate hereafter.

Section 8

Of the Passions Which Belong to Society

The other head under which I class our passions, is that of *society*, which may be divided into two sorts. 1. The society of the *sexes*, which answers the purpose of propagation; and next, that more *general society*, which we have with men and with other animals, and which we may in some sort be said to have even with the inanimate world. The passions belonging to the preservation of the individual turn wholly on pain and danger: those which belong to *generation* have their origin in gratifications and *pleasures*; the pleasure most directly belonging to this purpose is of a lively character, rapturous and violent, and confessedly the highest pleasure of sense; yet the absence of this so great an enjoyment scarce amounts to an uneasiness; and, except at particular times, I do not think it affects at all. When men describe in what manner they are affected by pain and danger, they do not dwell on the pleasure of health and the comfort of security, and then lament the *loss* of these satisfactions: the whole turns upon the actual pains and horrors which they endure. But if you listen to the complaints of a forsaken lover, you observe that he insists largely on the pleasures which he enjoyed, or hoped to enjoy, and on the perfection of the object of his desires; it is the *loss* which is always uppermost in his mind. The violent effects produced by love, which has sometimes been even wrought up to madness, is no objection to the rule which we seek to establish. When men have suffered their imaginations to be long affected with any idea, it so wholly engrosses them as to shut out by degrees almost every other, and to break down every partition of the mind which would confine it. Any idea is sufficient for the purpose, as is evident from the infinite variety of causes, which give rise to madness: but this at most can only prove, that the passion of love is capable of producing very extraordinary effects, not that its extraordinary emotions have any connection with positive pain.

Section 9

The Final Cause of the Difference Between the Passions Belonging to Self-Preservation and Those Which Regard the Society of the Sexes

The final cause of the difference in character between the passions which regard self-preservation, and those which are directed to the multiplication of the species, will illustrate the foregoing remarks yet further; and it is, I imagine, worthy of observation even upon its own account. As the performance of our duties of every kind depends upon life, and the performing them with vigor and efficacy depends upon health, we are very strongly affected with whatever threatens the destruction of either: but as we were not made to acquiesce in life and health, the simple enjoyment of them is not attended with any real pleasure, lest, satisfied with that, we should give ourselves over to indolence and inaction. On the other hand, the generation of mankind is a great purpose, and it is requisite that men should be animated to the pursuit of it by some great incentive. It is therefore attended with a very high pleasure; but as it is by no means designed to be our constant business, it is not fit that the absence of this pleasure should be attended with any considerable pain. The difference between men and brutes, in this point, seems to be remarkable. Men are at all times pretty equally disposed to the pleasures of love, because they are to be guided by reason in the time and manner of indulging them. Had any great pain arisen from the want of this satisfaction, reason, I am afraid, would find great difficulties in the performance of its office. But brutes that obey laws, in the execution of which their own reason has but little share, have their stated seasons; at such times it is not improbable that the sensation from the want is very troublesome, because the end must be then answered, or be missed in many, perhaps forever; as the inclination returns only with its season.

Section 10

OF BEAUTY

The passion which belongs to generation, merely as such, is lust only. This is evident in brutes, whose passions are more unmixed, and which pursue their purposes more directly than ours. The only distinction they observe with regard to their mates, is that of sex. It is true, that they stick severally to their own species in preference to all others. But this preference, I imagine, does not arise from any sense of beauty which they find in their species, as Mr. Addison supposes, but from a law of some other kind, to which they are subject; and this we may fairly conclude, from their apparent want of choice amongst those objects to which the barriers of their species have confined them. But man, who is a creature adapted to a greater variety and intricacy of relation, connects with the general passion the idea of some *social* qualities, which direct and heighten the appetite which he has in common with all other animals; and as he is not designed like them to live at large, it is fit that he should have something to create a preference, and fix his choice; and this in general should be some sensible quality; as no other can so quickly, so powerfully, or so surely produce its effect. The object therefore of this mixed passion, which we call love, is the *beauty* of the *sex*. Men are carried to the sex in general, as it is the sex, and by the common law of nature; but they are attached to particulars by personal *beauty*. I call beauty a social quality; for where women and men, and not only they, but when other animals give us a sense of joy and pleasure in beholding them (and there are many that do so), they inspire us with sentiments of tenderness and affection towards their persons; we like to have them near us, and we enter willingly into a kind of relation with them, unless we should have strong reasons to the contrary. But to what end, in many cases, this was designed, I am unable to discover; for I see no greater reason for a connection between man and several animals who are attired in so engaging a manner, than between him and some others who entirely want this attraction, or possess it in a far weaker degree. But it is probable that Providence did not make even this distinction, but with a view to some great end; though we cannot perceive distinctly what it is, as his wisdom is not our wisdom, nor our ways his ways.

Section 11

SOCIETY AND SOLITUDE

The second branch of the social passions is that which administers to *society in general*. With regard to this, I observe, that society, merely as society, without any particular heightenings, gives us no positive pleasure in the enjoyment; but absolute and entire *solitude*, that is, the total and perpetual exclusion from all society, is as great a positive pain as can almost be conceived. Therefore in the balance between the pleasure of general *society*, and the pain of absolute solitude, *pain* is the predominant idea. But the pleasure of any particular social enjoyment outweighs very considerably the uneasiness caused by the want of that particular enjoyment; so that the strongest sensations relative to the habitudes of *particular society* are sensations of pleasure. Good company, lively conversations, and the endearments of friendship, fill the mind with great pleasure; a temporary solitude, on the other hand, is itself agreeable. This may perhaps prove that we are creatures designed for contemplation as well as action; since solitude as well as society has its pleasures; as from the former observation we may discern, that an entire life of solitude contradicts the purposes of our being, since death itself is scarcely an idea of more terror.

Sympathy, Imitation, and Ambition

Under this denomination of society, the passions are of a complicated kind, and branch out into a variety of forms, agreeably to that variety of ends they are to serve in the great chain of society. The three principal links in this chain are *sympathy*, *imitation*, and *ambition*.

Section 13

Sympathy

It is by the first of these passions that we enter into the concerns of others; that we are moved as they are moved, and are never suffered to be indifferent spectators of almost anything which men can do or suffer. For sympathy must be considered as a sort of substitution, by which we are put into the place of another man, and affected in many respects as he is affected: so that this passion may either partake of the nature of those which regard self-preservation, and turning upon pain may be a source of the sublime; or it may turn upon ideas of pleasure; and then whatever has been said of the social affections, whether they regard society in general, or only some particular modes of it, may be applicable here. It is by this principle chiefly that poetry, painting, and other affecting arts, transfuse their passions from one breast to another, and are often capable of grafting a delight on wretchedness, misery, and death itself. It is a common observation, that objects which in the reality would shock, are in tragical, and such like representations, the source of a very high species of pleasure. This, taken as a fact, has been the cause of much reasoning. The satisfaction has been commonly attributed, first, to the comfort we receive in considering that so melancholy a story is no more than a fiction; and, next, to the contemplation of our own freedom from the evils which we see represented. I am afraid it is a practice much too common in inquiries of this nature, to attribute the cause of feelings which merely arise from the mechanical structure of our bodies, or from the natural frame and constitution of our minds, to certain conclusions of the reasoning faculty on the objects presented to us; for I should imagine, that the influence of reason in producing our passions is nothing near so extensive as it is commonly believed.

Section 14

THE EFFECTS OF SYMPATHY IN THE DISTRESSES OF OTHERS

To examine this point concerning the effect of tragedy in a proper manner, we must previously consider how we are affected by the feelings of our fellow creatures in circumstances of real distress. I am convinced we have a degree of delight, and that no small one, in the real misfortunes and pains of others; for let the affection be what it will in appearance, if it does not make us shun such objects, if on the contrary it induces us to approach them, if it makes us dwell upon them, in this case I conceive we must have a delight or pleasure of some species or other in contemplating objects of this kind. Do we not read the authentic histories of scenes of this nature with as much pleasure as romances or poems, where the incidents are fictitious? The prosperity of no empire, nor the grandeur of no king, can so agreeably affect in the reading, as the ruin of the state of Macedon, and the distress of its unhappy prince. Such a catastrophe touches us in history as much as the destruction of Troy does in fable. Our delight, in cases of this kind, is very greatly heightened, if the sufferer be some excellent person who sinks under an unworthy fortune. Scipio and Cato are both virtuous characters; but we are more deeply affected by the violent death of the one, and the ruin of the great cause he adhered to, than with the deserved triumphs and uninterrupted prosperity of the other: for terror is a passion which always produces delight when it does not press too closely; and pity is a passion accompanied with pleasure, because it arises from love and social affection. Whenever we are formed by nature to any active purpose, the passion which animates us to it is attended with delight, or a pleasure of some kind, let the subject-matter be what it will; and as our Creator has designed that we should be united by the bond of sympathy, he has strengthened that bond by a proportionable delight; and there most where our sympathy is most wanted,—in the distresses of others. If this passion was simply painful, we would shun with the greatest care all persons and places that could excite such a passion; as some, who are so far gone in indolence as not to endure any strong impression, actually do. But the case is widely different with the greater part of mankind;

EDMUND BURKE

there is no spectacle we so eagerly pursue, as that of some uncommon and grievous calamity; so that whether the misfortune is before our eyes, or whether they are turned back to it in history, it always touches with delight. This is not an unmixed delight, but blended with no small uneasiness. The delight we have in such things hinders us from shunning scenes of misery; and the pain we feel prompts us to relieve ourselves in relieving those who suffer; and all this antecedent to any reasoning, by an instinct that works us to its own purposes without our concurrence.

Section 15

OF THE EFFECTS OF TRAGEDY

It is thus in real calamities. In imitated distresses the only difference is the pleasure resulting from the effects of imitation; for it is never so perfect, but we can perceive it is imitation, and on that principle are somewhat pleased with it. And indeed in some cases we derive as much or more pleasure from that source than from the thing itself. But then I imagine we shall be much mistaken if we attribute any considerable part of our satisfaction in tragedy to the consideration that tragedy is a deceit, and its representations no realities. The nearer it approaches the reality, and the further it removes us from all idea of fiction, the more perfect is its power. But be its power of what kind it will, it never approaches to what it represents. Choose a day on which to represent the most sublime and affecting tragedy we have; appoint the most favorite actors; spare no cost upon the scenes and decorations; unite the greatest efforts of poetry, painting, and music; and when you have collected your audience, just at the moment when their minds are erect with expectation, let it be reported that a state criminal of high rank is on the point of being executed in the adjoining square; in a moment the emptiness of the theatre would demonstrate the comparative weakness of the imitative arts, and proclaim the triumph of the real sympathy. I believe that this notion of our having a simple pain in the reality, yet a delight in the representation, arises from hence, that we do not sufficiently distinguish what we would by no means choose to do, from what we should be eager enough to see if it was once done. We delight in seeing things, which so far from doing, our heartiest wishes would be to see redressed. This noble capital, the pride of England and of Europe, I believe no man is so strangely wicked as to desire to see destroyed by a conflagration or an earthquake, though he should be removed himself to the greatest distance from the danger. But suppose such a fatal accident to have happened, what numbers from all parts would crowd to behold the ruins, and amongst them many who would have been content never to have seen London in its glory! Nor is it, either in real or fictitious distresses, our immunity from them which produces our delight; in my own mind I can discover nothing like it. I apprehend that this mistake is owing to a sort of sophism, by which we are frequently imposed upon; it arises from our not distinguishing between what is indeed a necessary condition to our doing or suffering anything in general, and what is the *cause* of some particular act. If a man kills me with a sword, it is a necessary condition to this that we should have been both of us alive before the fact; and yet it would be absurd to say that our being both living creatures was the cause of his crime and of my death. So it is certain that it is absolutely necessary my life should be out of any imminent hazard, before I can take a delight in the sufferings of others, real or imaginary, or indeed in anything else from any cause whatsoever. But then it is a sophism to argue from thence that this immunity is the cause of my delight either on these or on any occasions. No one can distinguish such a cause of satisfaction in his own mind, I believe; nay, when we do not suffer any very acute pain, nor are exposed to any imminent danger of our lives, we can feel for others, whilst we suffer ourselves; and often then most when we are softened by affliction; we see with pity even distresses which we would accept in the place of our own.

Section 16

IMITATION

The second passion belonging to society is imitation, or, if you will, a desire of imitating, and consequently a pleasure in it. This passion arises from much the same cause with sympathy. For as sympathy makes us take a concern in whatever men feel, so this affection prompts us to copy whatever they do; and consequently we have a pleasure in imitating, and in whatever belongs to imitation merely as it is such, without any intervention of the reasoning faculty, but solely from our natural constitution, which Providence has framed in such a manner as to find either pleasure or delight, according to the nature of the object, in whatever regards the purposes of our being. It is by imitation far more than by precept, that we learn everything; and what we learn thus, we acquire not only more effectually, but more pleasantly. This forms our manners, our opinions, our lives. It is one of the strongest links of society; it is a species of mutual compliance, which all men yield to each other, without constraint to themselves, and which is extremely flattering to all. Herein it is that painting and many other agreeable arts have laid one of the principal foundations of their power. And since, by its influence on our manners and our passions, it is of such great consequence, I shall here venture to lay down a rule, which may inform us with a good degree of certainty when we are to attribute the power of the arts to imitation, or to our pleasure in the skill of the imitator merely, and when to sympathy, or some other cause in conjunction, with it. When the object represented in poetry or painting is such as we could have no desire of seeing in the reality, then I may be sure that its power in poetry or painting is owing to the power of imitation, and to no cause operating in the thing itself. So it is with most of the pieces which the painters call still-life. In these a cottage, a dung-hill, the meanest and most ordinary utensils of the kitchen, are capable of giving us pleasure. But when the object of the painting or poem is such as we should run to see if real, let it affect us with what odd sort of sense it will, we may rely upon it that the power of the poem or picture is more owing to the nature of the thing itself than to the mere effect of imitation, or to a consideration of the skill of the imitator, however excellent. Aristotle has spoken so much and so solidly upon the force of imitation in his Poetics, that it makes any further discourse upon this subject the less necessary.

Section 17

AMBITION

Although imitation is one of the great instruments used by Providence in bringing our nature towards its perfection, yet if men gave themselves up to imitation entirely, and each followed the other, and so on in an eternal circle, it is easy to see that there never could be any improvement amongst them. Men must remain as brutes do, the same at the end that they are at this day, and that they were in the beginning of the world. To prevent this, God has planted in man a sense of ambition, and a satisfaction arising from the contemplation of his excelling his fellows in something deemed valuable amongst them. It is this passion that drives men to all the ways we see in use of signalizing themselves, and that tends to make whatever excites in a man the idea of this distinction so very pleasant. It has been so strong as to make very miserable men take comfort, that they were supreme in misery; and certain it is that, where we cannot distinguish ourselves by something excellent, we begin to take a complacency in some singular infirmities, follies, or defects of one kind or other. It is on this principle that flattery is so prevalent; for flattery is no more than what raises in a man's mind an idea of a preference which he has not. Now, whatever, either on good or upon bad grounds, tends to raise a man in his own opinion, produces a sort of swelling and triumph, that is extremely grateful to the human mind; and this swelling is never more perceived, nor operates with more force, than when without danger we are conversant with terrible objects; the mind always claiming to itself some part of the dignity and importance of the things which it contemplates. Hence proceeds what Longinus has observed of that glorying and sense of inward greatness, that always fills the reader of such passages in poets and orators as are sublime: it is what every man must have felt in himself upon such occasions.

Section 18

THE RECAPITULATION

To draw the whole of what has been said into a few distinct points:—The passions which belong to self-preservation turn on pain and danger; they are simply painful when their causes immediately affect us; they are delightful when we have an idea of pain and danger, without being actually in such circumstances; this delight I have not called pleasure, because it turns on pain, and because it is different enough from any idea of positive pleasure. Whatever excites this delight, I call *sublime*. The passions belonging to self-preservation are the strongest of all the passions.

The second head to which the passions are referred with relation to their final cause, is society. There are two sorts of societies. The first is, the society of sex. The passion belonging to this is called love, and it contains a mixture of lust; its object is the beauty of women. The other is the great society with man and all other animals. The passion subservient to this is called likewise love, but it has no mixture of lust, and its object is beauty; which is a name I shall apply to all such qualities in things as induce in us a sense of affection and tenderness, or some other passion the most nearly resembling these. The passion of love has its rise in positive pleasure; it is, like all things which grow out of pleasure, capable of being mixed with a mode of uneasiness, that is, when an idea of its object is excited in the mind with an idea at the same time of having irretrievably lost it. This mixed sense of pleasure I have not called *pain*, because it turns upon actual pleasure, and because it is, both in its cause and in most of its effects, of a nature altogether different.

Next to the general passion we have for society, to a choice in which we are directed by the pleasure we have in the object, the particular passion under this head called sympathy has the greatest extent. The nature of this passion is, to put us in the place of another in whatever circumstance he is in, and to affect us in a like manner; so that this passion may, as the occasion requires, turn either on pain or pleasure; but with the modifications mentioned in some cases in Sect. 11. As to imitation and preference, nothing more need be said.

Section 19

The Conclusion

I believed that an attempt to range and methodize some of our most leading passions would be a good preparative to such an inquiry as we are going to make in the ensuing discourse. The passions I have mentioned are almost the only ones which it can be necessary to consider in our present design; though the variety of the passions is great, and worthy, in every branch of that variety, of an attentive investigation. The more accurately we search into the human mind, the stronger traces we everywhere find of His wisdom who made it. If a discourse on the use of the parts of the body may be considered as a hymn to the Creator; the use of the passions, which are the organs of the mind, cannot be barren of praise to him, nor unproductive to ourselves of that noble and uncommon union of science and admiration, which a contemplation of the works of infinite wisdom alone can afford to a rational mind; whilst, referring to him whatever we find of right or good or fair in ourselves, discovering his strength and wisdom even in our own weakness and imperfection, honoring them where we discover them clearly, and adoring their profundity where we are lost in our search, we may be inquisitive without impertinence, and elevated without pride; we may be admitted, if I may dare to say so, into the counsels of the Almighty by a consideration of his works. The elevation of the mind ought to be the principal end of all our studies; which, if they do not in some measure effect, they are of very little service to us. But, besides this great purpose, a consideration of the rationale of our passions seems to me very necessary for all who would affect them upon solid and sure principles. It is not enough to know them in general; to affect them after a delicate manner, or to judge properly of any work designed to affect them, we should know the exact boundaries of their several jurisdictions; we should pursue them through all their variety of operations, and pierce into the inmost, and what might appear inaccessible parts of our nature,

Quod latet arcanâ non enarrabile fibrâ.

Without all this it is possible for a man, after a confused manner sometimes to satisfy his own mind of the truth of his work; but he can never have a certain determinate rule to go by, nor can he ever make his propositions sufficiently clear to others. Poets, and orators, and painters, and those who cultivate other branches of the liberal arts, have, without this critical knowledge, succeeded well in their several provinces, and will succeed: as among artificers there are many machines made and even invented without any exact knowledge of the principles they are governed by. It is, I own, not uncommon to be wrong in theory, and right in practice: and we are happy that it is so. Men often act right from their feelings, who afterwards reason but ill on them from principle; but as it is impossible to avoid an attempt at such reasoning, and equally impossible to prevent its having some influence on our practice, surely it is worth taking some pains to have it just, and founded on the basis of sure experience. We might expect that the artists themselves would have been our surest guides; but the artists have been too much occupied in the practice: the philosophers have done little; and what they have done, was mostly with a view to their own schemes and systems; and as for those called critics, they have generally sought the rule of the arts in the wrong place; they sought it among poems, pictures, engravings, statues, and buildings. But art can never give the rules that make an art. This is, I believe, the reason why artists in general, and poets, principally, have been confined in so narrow a circle: they have been rather imitators of one another than of nature; and this with so faithful an uniformity, and to so remote an antiquity, that it is hard to say who gave the first model. Critics follow them, and therefore can do little as guides. I can judge but poorly of anything, whilst I measure it by no other standard than itself. The true standard of the arts is in every man's power; and an easy observation of the most common, sometimes of the meanest things in nature, will give the truest lights, where the greatest sagacity and industry, that slights such observation, must leave us in the dark, or, what is worse, amuse and mislead us by false lights. In an inquiry it is almost everything to be once in a right road. I am satisfied I have done but little by these observations considered in themselves; and I never should have taken the pains to digest them, much less should I have ever ventured to publish them, if I was not convinced that nothing tends more to the corruption of science than to suffer it to stagnate. These waters must be troubled, before they can exert their virtues. A man who works beyond the surface of things, though he may be wrong himself, yet he clears the way for others, and may chance to make even his errors subservient to the cause of truth. In the following parts I shall inquire what things they are that cause in us the affections of the sublime and beautiful, as in this I have considered the affections themselves. I only desire one favor,—that no part of this discourse may be judged of by itself, and independently of the rest; for I am sensible I have not disposed my materials to abide the test of a captious controversy, but of a sober and even forgiving examination; that they are not armed at all points for battle, but dressed to visit those who are willing to give a peaceful entrance to truth.

PART 2

Section 1

Of the Passion Caused by the Sublime

The passion caused by the great and sublime in *nature*, when those causes operate most powerfully, is astonishment: and astonishment is that state of the soul in which all its motions are suspended, with some degree of horror.[2] In this case the mind is so entirely filled with its object, that it cannot entertain any other, nor by consequence reason on that object which employs it. Hence arises the great power of the sublime, that, far from being produced by them, it anticipates our reasonings, and hurries us on by an irresistible force. Astonishment, as I have said, is the effect of the sublime in its highest degree; the inferior effects are admiration, reverence, and respect.

---

2. Part I. sect. 3, 4, 7.

Section 2

Terror

No passion so effectually robs the mind of all its powers of acting and reasoning as *fear*.[3] For fear being an apprehension of pain or death, it operates in a manner that resembles actual pain. Whatever therefore is terrible, with regard to sight, is sublime too, whether this cause of terror be endued with greatness of dimensions or not; for it is impossible to look on anything as trifling, or contemptible, that may be dangerous. There are many animals, who, though far from being large, are yet capable of raising ideas of the sublime, because they are considered as objects of terror. As serpents and poisonous animals of almost all kinds. And to things of great dimensions, if we annex an adventitious idea of terror, they become without comparison greater. A level plain of a vast extent on land, is certainly no mean idea; the prospect of such a plain may be as extensive as a prospect of the ocean; but can it ever fill the mind with anything so great as the ocean itself? This is owing to several causes; but it is owing to none more than this, that the ocean is an object of no small terror. Indeed terror is in all cases whatsoever, either more openly or latently, the ruling principle of the sublime. Several languages bear a strong testimony to the affinity of these ideas. They frequently use the same word to signify indifferently the modes of astonishment or admiration and those of terror. *Thambos* is in Greek either fear or wonder; *deinos* is terrible or respectable; *ahideo*, to reverence or to fear. *Vereor* in Latin is what *ahideo* is in Greek. The Romans used the verb *stupeo*, a term which strongly marks the state of an astonished mind, to express the effect either of simple fear, or of astonishment; the word *attonitus* (thunderstruck) is equally expressive of the alliance of these ideas; and do not the French *étonnement*, and the English *astonishment* and *amazement*, point out as clearly the kindred emotions which attend fear and wonder? They who have a more general knowledge of languages, could produce, I make no doubt, many other and equally striking examples.

---

3. Part IV. sect. 3, 4, 5, 6.

EDMUND BURKE

Section 3

OBSCURITY

To make anything very terrible, obscurity[4] seems in general to be necessary. When we know the full extent of any danger, when we can accustom our eyes to it, a great deal of the apprehension vanishes. Every one will be sensible of this, who considers how greatly night adds to our dread, in all cases of danger, and how much the notions of ghosts and goblins, of which none can form clear ideas, affect minds which give credit to the popular tales concerning such sorts of beings. Those despotic governments which are founded on the passions of men, and principally upon the passion of fear, keep their chief as much as may be from the public eye. The policy has been the same in many cases of religion. Almost all the heathen temples were dark. Even in the barbarous temples of the Americans at this day, they keep their idol in a dark part of the hut, which is consecrated to his worship. For this purpose too the Druids performed all their ceremonies in the bosom of the darkest woods, and in the shade of the oldest and most spreading oaks. No person seems better to have understood the secret of heightening, or of setting terrible things, if I may use the expression, in their strongest light, by the force of a judicious obscurity than Milton. His description of death in the second book is admirably studied; it is astonishing with what a gloomy pomp, with what a significant and expressive uncertainty of strokes and coloring, he has finished the portrait of the king of terrors:

> *"The other shape,*
> *If shape it might be called that shape had none*
> *Distinguishable, in member, joint, or limb;*
> *Or substance might be called that shadow seemed;*
> *For each seemed either; black he stood as night;*
> *Fierce as ten furies; terrible as hell;*
> *And shook a deadly dart. What seemed his head*
> *The likeness of a kingly crown had on."*

---

4. Part IV. sect. 14, 15, 16.

In this description all is dark, uncertain, confused, terrible, and sublime to the last degree.

Section 4

OF THE DIFFERENCE BETWEEN CLEARNESS AND OBSCURITY WITH REGARD TO THE PASSIONS

It is one thing to make an idea clear, and another to make it *affecting* to the imagination. If I make a drawing of a palace, or a temple, or a landscape, I present a very clear idea of those objects; but then (allowing for the effect of imitation which is something) my picture can at most affect only as the palace, temple, or landscape, would have affected in the reality. On the other hand, the most lively and spirited verbal description I can give raises a very obscure and imperfect *idea* of such objects; but then it is in my power to raise a stronger *emotion* by the description than I could do by the best painting. This experience constantly evinces. The proper manner of conveying the *affections* of the mind from one to another is by words; there is a great insufficiency in all other methods of communication; and so far is a clearness of imagery from being absolutely necessary to an influence upon the passions, that they may be considerably operated upon, without presenting any image at all, by certain sounds adapted to that purpose; of which we have a sufficient proof in the acknowledged and powerful effects of instrumental music. In reality, a great clearness helps but little towards affecting the passions, as it is in some sort an enemy to all enthusiasms whatsoever.

THERE ARE TWO VERSES IN Horace's Art of Poetry that seem to contradict this opinion; for which reason I shall take a little more pains in clearing it up. The verses are,

> *Segnius irritant animos demissa per aures,*
> *Quam quæ sunt oculis subjecta fidelibus.*

On this the Abbé du Bos founds a criticism, wherein he gives painting the preference to poetry in the article of moving the passions; principally on account of the greater *clearness* of the ideas it represents. I believe this excellent judge was led into this mistake (if it be a mistake) by his system; to which he found it more conformable than I imagine it will be found to experience. I know several who admire and love painting, and yet who regard the objects of their admiration in that art with coolness enough in comparison of that warmth with which they are animated by affecting pieces of poetry or rhetoric. Among the common sort of people, I never could perceive that painting had much influence on their passions. It is true that the best sorts of painting, as well as the best sorts of poetry, are not much understood in that sphere. But it is most certain that their passions are very strongly roused by a fanatic preacher, or by the ballads of Chevy Chase, or the Children in the Wood, and by other little popular poems and tales that are current in that rank of life. I do not know of any paintings, bad or good, that produce the same effect. So that poetry, with all its obscurity, has a more general, as well as a more powerful dominion over the passions, than the other art. And I think there are reasons in nature, why the obscure idea, when properly conveyed, should be more affecting than the clear. It is our ignorance of things that causes all our admiration, and chiefly excites our passions. Knowledge and acquaintance make the most striking causes affect but little. It is thus with the vulgar; and all men are as the vulgar in what they do not understand. The ideas of eternity, and infinity, are among the most affecting we have: and yet perhaps there is nothing of which we really understand so little, as of infinity and eternity. We do not anywhere meet a more sublime description than this justly-celebrated one of Milton, wherein he gives the portrait of Satan with a dignity so suitable to the subject:

> *"He above the rest*
> *In shape and gesture proudly eminent*
> *Stood like a tower; his form had yet not lost*
> *All her original brightness, nor appeared*
> *Less than archangel ruined, and th' excess*
> *Of glory obscured: as when the sun new risen*
> *Looks through the horizontal misty air*
> *Shorn of his beams; or from behind the moon*
> *In dim eclipse disastrous twilight sheds*
> *On half the nations; and with fear of change*
> *Perplexes monarchs."*

Here is a very noble picture; and in what does this poetical picture consist? In images of a tower, an archangel, the sun rising through mists, or in an eclipse, the ruin of monarchs and the revolutions of kingdoms. The mind is hurried out of itself, by a crowd of great and confused images; which affect because they are crowded and confused. For separate them, and you lose much of the greatness; and join them, and you infallibly lose the clearness. The images raised by poetry are always of this obscure kind; though in general the effects of poetry are by no means to be attributed to the images it raises; which point we shall examine more at large hereafter.[5] But painting, when we have allowed for the pleasure of imitation, can only affect simply by the images it presents; and even in painting, a judicious obscurity in some things contributes to the effect of the picture; because the images in painting are exactly similar to those in nature; and in nature, dark, confused, uncertain images have a greater power on the fancy to form the grander passions, than those have which are more clear and determinate. But where and when this observation may be applied to practice, and how far it shall be extended, will be better deduced from the nature of the subject, and from the occasion, than from any rules that can be given.

I am sensible that this idea has met with opposition, and is likely still to be rejected by several. But let it be considered that hardly anything can strike the mind with its greatness, which does not make some sort of approach towards infinity; which nothing can do whilst we are able to perceive its bounds; but to see an object distinctly, and to perceive its bounds, is one and the same thing. A clear idea is therefore another name for a little idea. There is a passage in the book of Job amazingly sublime, and this sublimity is principally due to the terrible uncertainty of the thing described: *In thoughts from the visions of the night, when deep sleep falleth upon men, fear came upon me and trembling, which made all my bones to shake. Then a spirit passed before my face. The hair of my flesh stood up. It stood still*, but I could not discern the form thereof; *an image was before mine eyes; there was silence; and I heard a voice,—Shall mortal man be more just than God?* We are first prepared with the utmost solemnity for the vision; we are first terrified, before we are let even into the obscure cause of our emotion: but when this grand cause of terror makes its appearance, what is it? Is it not wrapt up in the shades of its own incomprehensible darkness, more awful, more striking, more terrible, than the liveliest description, than the clearest painting, could possibly represent it? When painters have attempted to give us clear

5. Part V.

representations of these very fanciful and terrible ideas, they have, I think, almost always failed; insomuch that I have been at a loss, in all the pictures I have seen of hell, to determine whether the painter did not intend something ludicrous. Several painters have handled a subject of this kind, with a view of assembling as many horrid phantoms as their imagination could suggest; but all the designs I have chanced to meet of the temptations of St. Anthony were rather a sort of odd, wild grotesques, than any thing capable of producing a serious passion. In all these subjects poetry is very happy. Its apparitions, its chimeras, its harpies, its allegorical figures, are grand and affecting; and though Virgil's Fame and Homer's Discord are obscure, they are magnificent figures. These figures in painting would be clear enough, but I fear they might become ridiculous.

Section 5

Power

B esides those things which *directly* suggest the idea of danger, and those which produce a similar effect from a mechanical cause, I know of nothing sublime, which is not some modification of power. And this branch rises, as naturally as the other two branches, from terror, the common stock of everything that is sublime. The idea of power, at first view, seems of the class of those indifferent ones, which may equally belong to pain or to pleasure. But in reality, the affection arising from the idea of vast power is extremely remote from that neutral character. For first, we must remember[6] that the idea of pain, in its highest degree, is much stronger than the highest degree of pleasure; and that it preserves the same superiority through all the subordinate gradations. From hence it is, that where the chances for equal degrees of suffering or enjoyment are in any sort equal, the idea of the suffering must always be prevalent. And indeed the ideas of pain, and, above all, of death, are so very affecting, that whilst we remain in the presence of whatever is supposed to have the power of inflicting either, it is impossible to be perfectly free from terror. Again, we know by experience, that, for the enjoyment of pleasure, no great efforts of power are at all necessary; nay, we know that such efforts would go a great way towards destroying our satisfaction: for pleasure must be stolen, and not forced upon us; pleasure follows the will; and therefore we are generally affected with it by many things of a force greatly inferior to our own. But pain is always inflicted by a power in some way superior, because we never submit to pain willingly. So that strength, violence, pain, and terror, are ideas that rush in upon the mind together. Look at a man, or any other animal of prodigious strength, and what is your idea before reflection? Is it that this strength will be subservient to you, to your ease, to your pleasure, to your interest in any sense? No; the emotion you feel is, lest this enormous strength should be employed to the purposes of[7] rapine and destruction. That power derives all its sublimity from the terror with

---

6. Part I. sect. 7.
7. Vide Part III. sect. 21.

which it is generally accompanied, will appear evidently from its effect in the very few cases, in which it may be possible to strip a considerable degree of strength of its ability to hurt. When you do this, you spoil it of everything sublime, and it immediately becomes contemptible. An ox is a creature of vast strength; but he is an innocent creature, extremely serviceable, and not at all dangerous; for which reason the idea of an ox is by no means grand. A bull is strong too; but his strength is of another kind; often very destructive, seldom (at least amongst us) of any use in our business; the idea of a bull is therefore great, and it has frequently a place in sublime descriptions, and elevating comparisons. Let us look at another strong animal, in the two distinct lights in which we may consider him. The horse in the light of an useful beast, fit for the plough, the road, the draft; in every social useful light, the horse has nothing sublime; but is it thus that we are affected with him, *whose neck is clothed with thunder, the glory of whose nostrils is terrible, who swalloweth the ground with fierceness and rage, neither believeth that it is the sound of the trumpet*? In this description, the useful character of the horse entirely disappears, and the terrible and sublime blaze out together. We have continually about us animals of a strength that is considerable, but not pernicious. Amongst these we never look for the sublime; it comes upon us in the gloomy forest, and in the howling wilderness, in the form of the lion, the tiger, the panther, or rhinoceros. Whenever strength is only useful, and employed for our benefit or our pleasure, then it is never sublime; for nothing can act agreeably to us, that does not act in conformity to our will; but to act agreeably to our will, it must be subject to us, and therefore can never be the cause of a grand and commanding conception. The description of the wild ass, in Job, is worked up into no small sublimity, merely by insisting on his freedom, and his setting mankind at defiance; otherwise the description of such an animal could have had nothing noble in it. *Who hath loosed* (says he) *the bands of the wild ass? whose house I have made the wilderness and the barren land his dwellings. He scorneth the multitude of the city, neither regardeth he the voice of the driver. The range of the mountains is his pasture.* The magnificent description of the unicorn and of leviathan, in the same book, is full of the same heightening circumstances: *Will the unicorn be willing to serve thee? canst thou bind the unicorn with his band in the furrow? wilt thou trust him because his strength is great?—Canst thou draw out leviathan with an hook? will he make a covenant with thee? wilt thou take him for a servant forever? shall not one be cast down even at the sight of him?* In short, wheresoever we find strength, and in what light soever we look upon power, we shall all along observe the sublime the concomitant of terror, and contempt the attendant on a strength that is subservient and innoxious. The race of dogs, in many of their kinds, have generally a competent degree of strength and swiftness; and they exert these and other valuable qualities which they possess, greatly to our convenience and pleasure. Dogs are indeed the most social, affectionate, and amiable animals of the whole brute creation; but love approaches much nearer to contempt than is commonly imagined; and accordingly, though we caress dogs, we borrow from them an appellation of the most despicable kind, when we employ terms of reproach; and this appellation is the common mark of the last vileness and contempt in every language. Wolves have not more strength than several species of dogs; but, on account of their unmanageable fierceness, the idea of a wolf is not despicable; it is not excluded from grand descriptions and similitudes. Thus we are affected by strength, which is *natural* power. The power which arises from institution in kings and commanders, has the same connection with terror. Sovereigns are frequently addressed with the title of *dread majesty*. And it may be observed, that young persons, little acquainted with the world, and who have not been used to approach men in power, are commonly struck with an awe which takes away the free use of their faculties. *When I prepared my seat in the street,* (says Job,) *the young men saw me, and hid themselves.* Indeed so natural is this timidity with regard to power, and so strongly does it inhere in our constitution, that very few are able to conquer it, but by mixing much in the business of the great world, or by using no small violence to their natural dispositions. I know some people are of opinion, that no awe, no degree of terror, accompanies the idea of power; and have hazarded to affirm, that we can contemplate the idea of God himself without any such emotion. I purposely avoided, when I first considered this subject, to introduce the idea of that great and tremendous Being, as an example in an argument so light as this; though it frequently occurred to me, not as an objection to, but as a strong confirmation of, my notions in this matter. I hope, in what I am going to say, I shall avoid presumption, where it is almost impossible for any mortal to speak with strict propriety. I say then, that whilst we consider the Godhead merely as he is an object of the understanding, which forms a complex idea of power, wisdom, justice, goodness, all stretched to a degree far exceeding the bounds of our comprehension, whilst we consider the divinity in this refined and abstracted light, the imagination and passions are little or nothing affected. But because we are bound, by the condition of our nature, to ascend to these pure and intellectual ideas, through the medium of sensible images, and to judge of these divine qualities by their evident acts and exertions, it becomes extremely hard to disentangle our idea of the cause from the effect by which we are led to know it. Thus, when we contemplate the Deity, his attributes and their operation, coming united on the mind, form a sort of sensible image, and as such are capable of affecting the imagination. Now, though in a just idea of the Deity, perhaps none of his attributes are predominant, yet, to our imagination, his power is by far the most striking. Some reflection, some comparing, is necessary to satisfy us of his wisdom, his justice, and his goodness. To be struck with his power, it is only necessary that we should open our eyes. But whilst we contemplate so vast an object, under the arm, as it were, of almighty power, and invested upon every side with omnipresence, we shrink into the minuteness of our own nature, and are, in a manner, annihilated before him. And though a consideration of his other attributes may relieve, in some measure, our apprehensions; yet no conviction of the justice with which it is exercised, nor the mercy with which it is tempered, can wholly remove the terror that naturally arises from a force which nothing can withstand. If we rejoice, we rejoice with trembling; and even whilst we are receiving benefits, we cannot but shudder at a power which can confer benefits of such mighty importance. When the prophet David contemplated the wonders of wisdom and power which are displayed in the economy of man, he seems to be struck with a sort of divine horror, and cries out, *fearfully and wonderfully am I made*! An heathen poet has a sentiment of a similar nature; Horace looks upon it as the last effort of philosophical fortitude, to behold without terror and amazement, this immense and glorious fabric of the universe:

> *Hunc solem, et stellas, et decedentia certis*
> *Tempora momentis, sunt qui formidine nulla*
> *Imbuti spectent.*

Lucretius is a poet not to be suspected of giving way to superstitious terrors; yet, when he supposes the whole mechanism of nature laid open by the master of his philosophy, his transport on this magnificent view, which he has represented in the colors of such bold and lively poetry, is overcast with a shade of secret dread and horror:

> *His ibi me rebus quædam divina voluptas*
> *Percipit, atque horror; quod sic natura, tua vi*
> *Tam manifesta patens, ex omni parte retecta est.*

But the Scripture alone can supply ideas answerable to the majesty of this subject. In the Scripture, wherever God is represented as appearing or speaking, everything terrible in nature is called up to heighten the awe and solemnity of the Divine presence. The Psalms, and the prophetical books, are crowded with instances of this kind. *The earth shook,* (says the Psalmist,) *the heavens also dropped at the presence of the Lord.* And what is remarkable, the painting preserves the same character, not only when he is supposed descending to take vengeance upon the wicked, but even when he exerts the like plenitude of power in acts of beneficence to mankind. *Tremble, thou earth! at the presence of the Lord; at the presence of the God of Jacob; which turned the rock into standing water, the flint into a fountain of waters!* It were endless to enumerate all the passages, both in the sacred and profane writers, which establish the general sentiment of mankind, concerning the inseparable union of a sacred and reverential awe, with our ideas of the divinity. Hence the common maxim, *Primus in orbe deos fecit timor.* This maxim may be, as I believe it is, false with regard to the origin of religion. The maker of the maxim saw how inseparable these ideas were, without considering that the notion of some great power must be always precedent to our dread of it. But this dread must necessarily follow the idea of such a power, when it is once excited in the mind. It is on this principle that true religion has, and must have, so large a mixture of salutary fear; and that false religions have generally nothing else but fear to support them. Before the Christian religion had, as it were, humanized the idea of the Divinity, and brought it somewhat nearer to us, there was very little said of the love of God. The followers of Plato have something of it, and only something; the other writers of pagan antiquity, whether poets or philosophers, nothing at all. And they who consider with what infinite attention, by what a disregard of every perishable object, through what long habits of piety and contemplation it is that any man is able to attain an entire love and devotion to the Deity, will easily perceive that it is not the first, the most natural, and the most striking effect which proceeds from that idea. Thus we have traced power through its several gradations unto the highest of all, where our imagination is finally lost; and we find terror, quite throughout the progress, its inseparable companion, and growing along with it, as far as we can possibly trace them. Now, as power is undoubtedly a capital source of the sublime, this will point out evidently from whence its energy is derived, and to what class of ideas we ought to unite it.

Section 6

PRIVATION

All *general* privations are great, because they are all terrible; *vacuity, darkness, solitude,* and *silence*. With what a fire of imagination, yet with what severity of judgment, has Virgil amassed all these circumstances, where he knows that all the images of a tremendous dignity ought to be united at the mouth of hell! Where, before he unlocks the secrets of the great deep, he seems to be seized with a religious horror, and to retire astonished at the boldness of his own design:

> *Dii, quibus imperium est animarum, umbræque* silentes*!*
> *Et Chaos, et Phlegethon! loca* nocte silentia *late!*
> *Sit mihi fas audita loqui! sit numine vestro*
> *Pandere res alta terra et* caligine *mersas!*
> *Ibant* obscuri, sola *sub* nocte, *per* umbram,
> *Perque domos Ditis* vacuas, *et* inania *regus.*

> *"Ye subterraneous gods! whose awful sway*
> *The gliding ghosts, and* silent *shades obey:*
> *O Chaos hoar! and Phlegethon profound!*
> *Whose solemn empire stretches wide around;*
> *Give me, ye great, tremendous powers, to tell*
> *Of scenes and wonders in the depth of hell;*
> *Give me your mighty secrets to display*
> *From those* black *realms of darkness to the day."*

> —PITT

> *"Obscure they went through dreary shades that led*
> *Along the waste dominions of the dead."*

> —DRYDEN

VASTNESS

Greatness[8] of dimension is a powerful cause of the sublime. This is too evident, and the observation too common, to need any illustration; it is not so common to consider in what ways greatness of dimension, vastness of extent or quantity, has the most striking effect. For, certainly, there are ways and modes wherein the same quantity of extension shall produce greater effects than it is found to do in others. Extension is either in length, height, or depth. Of these the length strikes least; a hundred yards of even ground will never work such an effect as a tower a hundred yards high, or a rock or mountain of that altitude. I am apt to imagine, likewise, that height is less grand than depth; and that we are more struck at looking down from a precipice, than looking up at an object of equal height; but of that I am not very positive. A perpendicular has more force in forming the sublime, than an inclined plane, and the effects of a rugged and broken surface seem stronger than where it is smooth and polished. It would carry us out of our way to enter in this place into the cause of these appearances, but certain it is they afford a large and fruitful field of speculation. However, it may not be amiss to add to these remarks upon magnitude, that as the great extreme of dimension is sublime, so the last extreme of littleness is in some measure sublime likewise; when we attend to the infinite divisibility of matter, when we pursue animal life into these excessively small, and yet organized beings, that escape the nicest inquisition of the sense; when we push our discoveries yet downward, and consider those creatures so many degrees yet smaller, and the still diminishing scale of existence, in tracing which the imagination is lost as well as the sense; we become amazed and confounded at the wonders of minuteness; nor can we distinguish in its effect this extreme of littleness from the vast itself. For division must be infinite as well as addition; because the idea of a perfect unity can no more be arrived at, than that of a complete whole, to which nothing may be added.

---

8. Part IV. sect. 9.

Section 8

INFINITY

Another source of the sublime is *infinity*; if it does not rather belong to the last. Infinity has a tendency to fill the mind with that sort of delightful horror, which is the most genuine effect, and truest test of the sublime. There are scarce any things which can become the objects of our senses, that are really and in their own nature infinite. But the eye not being able to perceive the bounds of many things, they seem to be infinite, and they produce the same effects as if they were really so. We are deceived in the like manner, if the parts of some large object are so continued to any indefinite number, that the imagination meets no check which may hinder its extending them at pleasure.

Whenever we repeat any idea frequently, the mind, by a sort of mechanism, repeats it long after the first cause has ceased to operate.[9] After whirling about, when we sit down, the objects about us still seem to whirl. After a long succession of noises, as the fall of waters, or the beating of forge-hammers, the hammers beat and the waters roar in the imagination long after the first sounds have ceased to affect it; and they die away at last by gradations which are scarcely perceptible. If you hold up a straight pole, with your eye to one end, it will seem extended to a length almost incredible.[10] Place a number of uniform and equidistant marks on this pole, they will cause the same deception, and seem multiplied without end. The senses, strongly affected in some one manner, cannot quickly change their tenor, or adapt themselves to other things; but they continue in their old channel until the strength of the first mover decays. This is the reason of an appearance very frequent in madmen; that they remain whole days and nights, sometimes whole years, in the constant repetition of some remark, some complaint, or song; which having struck powerfully on their disordered imagination, in the beginning of their frenzy, every repetition reinforces it with new strength, and the hurry of their spirits, unrestrained by the curb of reason, continues it to the end of their lives.

---

9. Part IV. sect. 11.
10. Part IV. sect. 13.

Section 9

Succession and Uniformity

Succession and *uniformity* of parts are what constitute the artificial infinite. 1. *Succession*; which is requisite that the parts may be continued so long and in such a direction, as by their frequent impulses on the sense to impress the imagination with an idea of their progress beyond their actual limits. 2. *Uniformity*; because, if the figures of the parts should be changed, the imagination at every change finds a check; you are presented at every alteration with the termination of one idea, and the beginning of another; by which means it becomes impossible to continue that uninterrupted progression, which alone can stamp on bounded objects the character of infinity. It is in this kind of artificial infinity, I believe, we ought to look for the cause why a rotund has such a noble effect.[11] For in a rotund, whether it be a building or a plantation, you can nowhere fix a boundary; turn which way you will, the same object still seems to continue, and the imagination has no rest. But the parts must be uniform, as well as circularly disposed, to give this figure its full force; because any difference, whether it be in the disposition, or in the figure, or even in the color of the parts, is highly prejudicial to the idea of infinity, which every change must check and interrupt, at every alteration commencing a new series. On the same principles of succession and uniformity, the grand appearance of the ancient heathen temples, which were generally oblong forms, with a range of uniform pillars on every side, will be easily accounted for. From the same cause also may be derived the grand effect of the aisles in many of our own old cathedrals. The form of a cross used in some churches seems to me not so eligible as the parallelogram of the ancients; at least, I imagine it is not so proper for the outside. For, supposing the arms of the cross every way equal, if you stand in a direction parallel to any of the side walls, or colonnades, instead of a deception that makes the building more extended than it is, you are cut off from a considerable part (two thirds) of its *actual* length;

---

11. Mr. Addison, in the Spectators concerning the pleasures of the imagination, thinks it is because in the rotund at one glance you see half the building. This I do not imagine to be the real cause.

EDMUND BURKE

and, to prevent all possibility of progression, the arms of the cross taking a new direction, make a right angle with the beam, and thereby wholly turn the imagination from the repetition of the former idea. Or suppose the spectator placed where he may take a direct view of such a building, what will be the consequence? the necessary consequence will be, that a good part of the basis of each angle formed by the intersection of the arms of the cross, must be inevitably lost; the whole must of course assume a broken, unconnected figure; the lights must be unequal, here strong, and there weak; without that noble gradation which the perspective always effects on parts disposed uninterruptedly in a right line. Some or all of these objections will lie against every figure of a cross, in whatever view you take it. I exemplified them in the Greek cross, in which these faults appear the most strongly; but they appear in some degree in all sorts of crosses. Indeed, there is nothing more prejudicial to the grandeur of buildings than to abound in angles; a fault obvious in many; and owing to an inordinate thirst for variety, which, whenever it prevails, is sure to leave very little true taste.

Section 10

Magnitude in Building

To the sublime in building, greatness of dimension seems requisite; for on a few parts, and those small, the imagination cannot rise to any idea of infinity. No greatness in the manner can effectually compensate for the want of proper dimensions. There is no danger of drawing men into extravagant designs by this rule; it carries its own caution along with it. Because too great a length in buildings destroys the purpose of greatness, which it was intended to promote; the perspective will lessen it in height as it gains in length; and will bring it at last to a point; turning the whole figure into a sort of triangle, the poorest in its effect of almost any figure that can be presented to the eye. I have ever observed, that colonnades and avenues of trees of a moderate length were, without comparison, far grander than when they were suffered to run to immense distances. A true artist should put a generous deceit on the spectators, and effect the noblest designs by easy methods. Designs that are vast only by their dimensions are always the sign of a common and low imagination. No work of art can be great, but as it deceives; to be otherwise is the prerogative of nature only. A good eye will fix the medium betwixt an excessive length or height (for the same objection lies against both), and a short or broken quantity: and perhaps it might be ascertained to a tolerable degree of exactness, if it was my purpose to descend far into the particulars of any art.

Section 11

INFINITY IN PLEASING OBJECTS

Infinity, though of another kind, causes much of our pleasure in agreeable, as well as of our delight in sublime images. The spring is the pleasantest of the seasons; and the young of most animals, though far from being completely fashioned, afford a more agreeable sensation than the full-grown; because the imagination is entertained with the promise of something more, and does not acquiesce in the present object of the sense. In unfinished sketches of drawing, I have often seen something which pleased me beyond the best finishing; and this I believe proceeds from the cause I have just now assigned.

DIFFICULTY

A nother source of greatness is *difficulty*.[12] When any work seems to have required immense force and labor to effect it, the idea is grand. Stonehenge, neither for disposition nor ornament, has anything admirable; but those huge rude masses of stone, set on end, and piled each on other, turn the mind on the immense force necessary for such a work. Nay, the rudeness of the work increases this cause of grandeur, as it excludes the idea of art and contrivance; for dexterity produces another sort of effect, which is different enough from this.

---

12. Part IV. sect. 4, 5, 6.

Section 13

Magnificence

Magnificence is likewise a source of the sublime. A great profusion of things, which are splendid or valuable in themselves, is *magnificent*. The starry heaven, though it occurs so very frequently to our view never fails to excite an idea of grandeur. This cannot be owing to the stars themselves, separately considered. The number is certainly the cause. The apparent disorder augments the grandeur, for the appearance of care is highly contrary to our ideas of magnificence. Besides, the stars lie in such apparent confusion, as makes it impossible on ordinary occasions to reckon them. This gives them the advantage of a sort of infinity. In works of art, this kind of grandeur which consists in multitude, is to be very cautiously admitted; because a profusion of excellent things is not to be attained, or with too much difficulty; and because in many cases this splendid confusion would destroy all use, which should be attended to in most of the works of art with the greatest care; besides, it is to be considered, that unless you can produce an appearance of infinity by your disorder, you will have disorder only without magnificence. There are, however, a sort of fireworks, and some other things, that in this way succeed well, and are truly grand. There are also many descriptions in the poets and orators, which owe their sublimity to a richness and profusion of images, in which the mind is so dazzled as to make it impossible to attend to that exact coherence and agreement of the allusions, which we should require on every other occasion. I do not now remember a more striking example of this, than the description which is given of the king's army in the play of Henry IV:—

> *"All furnished, all in arms,*
> *All plumed like ostriches that with the wind*
> *Baited like eagles having lately bathed:*
> *As full of spirit us the month of May,*
> *And gorgeous as the sun in midsummer,*
> *Wanton as youthful goats, wild as young bulls.*
> *I saw young Harry with his beaver on*
> *Rise from the ground like feathered Mercury;*

> *And vaulted with such ease into his seat,*
> *As if an angel dropped down from the clouds*
> *To turn and wind a fiery Pegasus."*

In that excellent book, so remarkable for the vivacity of its descriptions, as well as the solidity and penetration of its sentences, the Wisdom of the Son of Sirach, there is a noble panegyric on the high-priest Simon the son of Onias; and it is a very fine example of the point before us:—

> *How was he honored in the midst of the people, in his coming out of the sanctuary! He was as the morning star in the midst of a cloud, and as the moon at the full; as the sun shining upon the temple of the Most High, and as the rainbow giving light in the bright clouds: and as the flower of roses in the spring of the year, as lilies by the rivers of waters, and as the frankincense-tree in summer; as fire and incense in the censer, and as a vessel of gold set with precious stones; as a fair olive-tree budding forth fruit, and as a cypress which groweth up to the clouds. When he put on the robe of honor, and was clothed with the perfection of glory, when he went up to the holy altar, he made the garment of holiness honorable. He himself stood by the hearth of the altar, compassed with his brethren round about; as a young cedar in Libanus, and as palm-trees compassed they him about. So were all the sons of Aaron in their glory, and the oblations of the Lord in their hands, &c.*

Section 14

LIGHT

Having considered extension, so far as it is capable of raising ideas of greatness; *color* comes next under consideration. All colors depend on *light*. Light therefore ought previously to be examined; and with it its opposite, darkness. With regard to light, to make it a cause capable of producing the sublime, it must be attended with some circumstances, besides its bare faculty of showing other objects. Mere light is too common a thing to make a strong impression on the mind, and without a strong impression nothing can be sublime. But such a light as that of the sun, immediately exerted on the eye, as it overpowers the sense, is a very great idea. Light of an inferior strength to this, if it moves with great celerity, has the same power; for lightning is certainly productive of grandeur, which it owes chiefly to the extreme velocity of its motion. A quick transition from light to darkness, or from darkness to light, has yet a greater effect. But darkness is more productive of sublime ideas than light. Our great poet was convinced of this; and indeed so full was he of this idea, so entirely possessed with the power of a well-managed darkness, that in describing the appearance of the Deity, amidst that profusion of magnificent images, which the grandeur of his subject provokes him to pour out upon every side, he is far from forgetting the obscurity which surrounds the most incomprehensible of all beings, but

> *"With majesty of* darkness *round*
> *Circles his throne."*

And what is no less remarkable, our author had the secret of preserving this idea, even when he seemed to depart the farthest from it, when he describes the light and glory which flows from the Divine presence; a light which by its very excess is converted into a species of darkness:—

> *"*Dark *with excessive* light *thy skirts appear."*

Here is an idea not only poetical in a high degree, but strictly and philosophically just. Extreme light, by overcoming the organs of sight, obliterates all objects, so as in its effect exactly to resemble darkness. After looking for some time at the sun, two black spots, the impression which it leaves, seem to dance before our eyes. Thus are two ideas as opposite as can be imagined reconciled in the extremes of both; and both, in spite of their opposite nature, brought to concur in producing the sublime. And this is not the only instance wherein the opposite extremes operate equally in favor of the sublime, which in all things abhors mediocrity.

Section 15

LIGHT IN BUILDING

As the management of light is a matter of importance in architecture, it is worth inquiring, how far this remark is applicable to building. I think, then, that all edifices calculated to produce an idea of the sublime, ought rather to be dark and gloomy, and this for two reasons; the first is, that darkness itself on other occasions is known by experience to have a greater effect on the passions than light. The second is, that to make an object very striking, we should make it as different as possible from the objects with which we have been immediately conversant; when therefore you enter a building, you cannot pass into a greater light than you had in the open air; to go into one some few degrees less luminous, can make only a trifling change; but to make the transition thoroughly striking, you ought to pass from the greatest light, to as much darkness as is consistent with the uses of architecture. At night the contrary rule will hold, but for the very same reason; and the more highly a room is then illuminated, the grander will the passion be.

Section 16

Color Considered as Productive of the Sublime

Among colors, such as are soft or cheerful (except perhaps a strong red, which is cheerful) are unfit to produce grand images. An immense mountain covered with a shining green turf, is nothing, in this respect, to one dark and gloomy; the cloudy sky is more grand than the blue; and night more sublime and solemn than day. Therefore in historical painting, a gay or gaudy drapery can never have a happy effect: and in buildings, when the highest degree of the sublime is intended, the materials and ornaments ought neither to be white, nor green, nor yellow, nor blue, nor of a pale red, nor violet, nor spotted, but of sad and fuscous colors, as black, or brown, or deep purple, and the like. Much of gilding, mosaics, painting, or statues, contribute but little to the sublime. This rule need not be put in practice, except where an uniform degree of the most striking sublimity is to be produced, and that in every particular; for it ought to be observed, that this melancholy kind of greatness, though it be certainly the highest, ought not to be studied in all sorts of edifices, where yet grandeur must be studied; in such cases the sublimity must be drawn from the other sources; with a strict caution however against anything light and riant; as nothing so effectually deadens the whole taste of the sublime.

Section 17

Sound and Loudness

The eye is not the only organ of sensation by which a sublime passion may be produced. Sounds have a great power in these as in most other passions. I do not mean words, because words do not affect simply by their sounds, but by means altogether different. Excessive loudness alone is sufficient to overpower the soul, to suspend its action, and to fill it with terror. The noise of vast cataracts, raging storms, thunder, or artillery, awakes a great and awful sensation in the mind, though we can observe no nicety or artifice in those sorts of music. The shouting of multitudes has a similar effect; and by the sole strength of the sound, so amazes and confounds the imagination, that, in this staggering and hurry of the mind, the best established tempers can scarcely forbear being borne down, and joining in the common cry, and common resolution of the crowd.

SUDDENNESS

A sudden beginning, or sudden cessation of sound of any considerable force, has the same power. The attention is roused by this; and the faculties driven forward, as it were, on their guard. Whatever, either in sights or sounds, makes the transition from one extreme to the other easy, causes no terror, and consequently can be no cause of greatness. In everything sudden and unexpected, we are apt to start; that is, we have a perception of danger, and our nature rouses us to guard against it. It may be observed that a single sound of some strength, though but of short duration, if repeated after intervals, has a grand effect. Few things are more awful than the striking of a great clock, when the silence of the night prevents the attention from being too much dissipated. The same may be said of a single stroke on a drum, repeated with pauses; and of the successive firing of cannon at a distance. All the effects mentioned in this section have causes very nearly alike.

Section 19

Intermitting

A low, tremulous, intermitting sound, though it seems, in some respects, opposite to that just mentioned, is productive of the sublime. It is worth while to examine this a little. The fact itself must be determined by every man's own experience and reflection. I have already observed, that night[13] increases our terror, more perhaps than anything else; it is our nature, when we do not know what may happen to us, to fear the worst that can happen; and hence it is that uncertainty is so terrible, that we often seek to be rid of it, at the hazard of a certain mischief. Now some low, confused, uncertain sounds, leave us in the same fearful anxiety concerning their causes, that no light, or an uncertain light, does concerning the objects that surround us.

> *Quale per incertam lunam sub luce maligna*
> *Est iter in sylvis.*

> *"A faint shadow of uncertain light,*
> *Like as a lamp, whose life doth fade away;*
> *Or as the moon clothed with cloudy night*
> *Doth show to him who walks in fear and great affright."*

> —Spenser

But light now appearing, and now leaving us, and so off and on, is even more terrible than total darkness; and a sort of uncertain sounds are, when the necessary dispositions concur, more alarming than a total silence.

---

13. Sect. 3.

Section 20

The Cries of Animals

S uch sounds as imitate the natural inarticulate voices of men, or any animals in pain or danger, are capable of conveying great ideas; unless it be the well-known voice of some creature, on which we are used to look with contempt. The angry tones of wild beasts are equally capable of causing a great and awful sensation.

> *Hinc exaudiri gemitus, iræque leonum*
> *Vincla recusantum, et sera sub nocte rudentum;*
> *Setigerique sues, atque in præsepibus ursi*
> *Sævire; et formæ magnorum ululare luporam.*

It might seem that those modulations of sound carry some connection with the nature of the things they represent, and are not merely arbitrary; because the natural cries of all animals, even of those animals with whom we have not been acquainted, never fail to make themselves sufficiently understood; this cannot be said of language. The modifications of sound, which may be productive of the sublime, are almost infinite. Those I have mentioned are only a few instances to show on what principles they are all built.

Section 21

SMELL AND TASTE—BITTERS AND STENCHES

Smells and *tastes* have some share too in ideas of greatness; but it is a small one, weak in its nature, and confined in its operations. I shall only observe that no smells or tastes can produce a grand sensation, except excessive bitters, and intolerable stenches. It is true that these affections of the smell and taste, when they are in their full force, and lean directly upon the sensory, are simply painful, and accompanied with no sort of delight; but when they are moderated, as in a description or narrative, they become sources of the sublime, as genuine as any other, and upon the very same principle of a moderated pain. "A cup of bitterness"; "to drain the bitter cup of fortune"; "the bitter apples of Sodom"; these are all ideas suitable to a sublime description. Nor is this passage of Virgil without sublimity, where the stench of the vapor in Albunea conspires so happily with the sacred horror and gloominess of that prophetic forest:

> *At rex sollicitus monstris oracula Fauni*
> *Fatidici genitoris adit, lucosque sub alta*
> *Consulit Albunea, nemorum quæ maxima sacro*
> *Fonte sonat;* sævamque exhalat opaca Mephitim.

In the sixth book, and in a very sublime description, the poisonous exhalation of Acheron is not forgotten, nor does it at all disagree with the other images amongst which it is introduced:

> *Spelunca* alta *fuit,* vastoque immanis *hiatu*
> *Scrupea, tuta* lacu nigro, *nemorumque* tenebris;
> *Quam super haud ullæ poterant impune volantes*
> *Tendere iter pennis:* talis sese halitus atris
> Faucibus effundens supera ad convexa ferebat.

I have added these examples, because some friends, for whose judgment I have great deference, were of opinion that if the sentiment stood nakedly by itself, it would be subject, at first view, to burlesque and ridicule; but this I imagine would principally arise from considering the bitterness and stench in company with mean and contemptible ideas, with which it must be owned they are often united; such an union degrades the sublime in all other instances as well as in those. But it is one of the tests by which the sublimity of an image is to be tried, not whether it becomes mean when associated with mean ideas; but whether, when united with images of an allowed grandeur, the whole composition is supported with dignity. Things which are terrible are always great; but when things possess disagreeable qualities, or such as have indeed some degree of danger, but of a danger easily overcome, they are merely *odious*; as toads and spiders.

Section 22

Feeling—Pain

Of *feeling* little more can be said than that the idea of bodily pain, in all the modes and degrees of labor, pain, anguish, torment, is productive of the sublime; and nothing else in this sense can produce it. I need not give here any fresh instances, as those given in the former sections abundantly illustrate a remark that, in reality, wants only an attention to nature, to be made by everybody.

Having thus run through the causes of the sublime with reference to all the senses, my first observation (Sect. 7) will be found very nearly true; that the sublime is an idea belonging to self-preservation; that it is, therefore, one of the most affecting we have; that its strongest emotion is an emotion of distress; and that no pleasure[14] from a positive cause belongs to it. Numberless examples, besides those mentioned, might be brought in support of these truths, and many perhaps useful consequences drawn from them—

> *Sed fugit interea, fugit irrevocabile tempus,*
> *Singula dum capti circumvectamur amore.*

---

14. Vide Part I. sect. 6.

PART 3

Section 1

OF BEAUTY

It is my design to consider beauty as distinguished from the sublime; and, in the course of the inquiry, to examine how far it is consistent with it. But previous to this, we must take a short review of the opinions already entertained of this quality; which I think are hardly to be reduced to any fixed principles; because men are used to talk of beauty in a figurative manner, that is to say, in a manner extremely uncertain, and indeterminate. By beauty, I mean that quality, or those qualities in bodies, by which they cause love, or some passion similar to it. I confine this definition to the merely sensible qualities of things, for the sake of preserving the utmost simplicity in a subject, which must always distract us whenever we take in those various causes of sympathy which attach us to any persons or things from secondary considerations, and not from the direct force which they have merely on being viewed. I likewise distinguish love, (by which I mean that satisfaction which arises to the mind upon contemplating anything beautiful, of whatsoever nature it may be,) from desire or lust; which is an energy of the mind, that hurries us on to the possession of certain objects, that do not affect us as they are beautiful, but by means altogether different. We shall have a strong desire for a woman of no remarkable beauty; whilst the greatest beauty in men, or in other animals, though it causes love, yet excites nothing at all of desire. Which shows that beauty, and the passion caused by beauty, which I call love, is different from desire, though desire may sometimes operate along with it; but it is to this latter that we must attribute those violent and tempestuous passions, and the consequent emotions of the body which attend what is called love in some of its ordinary acceptations, and not to the effects of beauty merely as it is such.

Section 2

PROPORTION NOT THE CAUSE OF
BEAUTY IN VEGETABLES

B eauty hath usually been said to consist in certain proportions of
parts. On considering the matter, I have great reason to doubt,
whether beauty be at all an idea belonging to proportion. Proportion
relates almost wholly to convenience, as every idea of order seems to do;
and it must therefore be considered as a creature of the understanding,
rather than a primary cause acting on the senses and imagination. It is
not by the force of long attention and inquiry that we find any object
to be beautiful; beauty demands no assistance from our reasoning; even
the will is unconcerned; the appearance of beauty as effectually causes
some degree of love in us, as the application of ice or fire produces the
ideas of heat or cold. To gain something like a satisfactory conclusion
in this point, it were well to examine what proportion is; since several
who make use of that word do not always seem to understand very
clearly the force of the term, nor to have very distinct ideas concerning
the thing itself. Proportion is the measure of relative quantity. Since
all quantity is divisible, it is evident that every distinct part into which
any quantity is divided must bear some relation to the other parts, or to
the whole. These relations give an origin to the idea of proportion. They
are discovered by mensuration, and they are the objects of mathematical
inquiry. But whether any part of any determinate quantity be a fourth,
or a fifth, or a sixth, or a moiety of the whole; or whether it be of equal
length with any other part, or double its length, or but one half, is a
matter merely indifferent to the mind; it stands neuter in the question:
and it is from this absolute indifference and tranquillity of the mind,
that mathematical speculations derive some of their most considerable
advantages; because there is nothing to interest the imagination;
because the judgment sits free and unbiassed to examine the point. All
proportions, every arrangement of quantity, is alike to the understanding,
because the same truths result to it from all; from greater, from lesser,
from equality and inequality. But surely beauty is no idea belonging to
mensuration; nor has it anything to do with calculation and geometry. If
it had, we might then point out some certain measures which we could

demonstrate to be beautiful, either as simply considered, or as related to others; and we could call in those natural objects, for whose beauty we have no voucher but the sense, to this happy standard, and confirm the voice of our passions by the determination of our reason. But since we have not this help, let us see whether proportion can in any sense be considered as the cause of beauty, as hath been so generally, and, by some, so confidently affirmed. If proportion be one of the constituents of beauty, it must derive that power either from some natural properties inherent in certain measures, which operate mechanically; from the operation of custom; or from the fitness which some measures have to answer some particular ends of conveniency. Our business therefore is to inquire, whether the parts of those objects, which are found beautiful in the vegetable or animal kingdoms, are constantly so formed according to such certain measures, as may serve to satisfy us that their beauty results from those measures, on the principle of a natural mechanical cause; or from custom; or, in fine, from their fitness for any determinate purposes. I intend to examine this point under each of these heads in their order. But before I proceed further, I hope it will not be thought amiss, if I lay down the rules which governed me in this inquiry, and which have misled me in it, if I have gone astray. 1. If two bodies produce the same or a similar effect on the mind, and on examination they are found to agree in some of their properties, and to differ in others; the common effect is to be attributed to the properties in which they agree, and not to those in which they differ. 2. Not to account for the effect of a natural object from the effect of an artificial object. 3. Not to account for the effect of any natural object from a conclusion of our reason concerning its uses, if a natural cause may be assigned. 4. Not to admit any determinate quantity, or any relation of quantity, as the cause of a certain effect, if the effect is produced by different or opposite measures and relations; or if these measures and relations may exist, and yet the effect may not be produced. These are the rules which I have chiefly followed, whilst I examined into the power of proportion considered as a natural cause; and these, if he thinks them just, I request the reader to carry with him throughout the following discussion; whilst we inquire, in the first place, in what things we find this quality of beauty; next, to see whether in these we can find any assignable proportions in such a manner as ought to convince us that our idea of beauty results from them. We shall consider this pleasing power as it appears in vegetables, in the inferior animals, and in man. Turning our eyes to the vegetable creation, we find nothing there so beautiful as flowers; but flowers are almost of every sort of shape, and of every sort of disposition; they are turned and fashioned into an infinite variety of forms; and from these forms botanists have given them their names, which are almost as various. What proportion do we discover between the stalks and the leaves of flowers, or between the leaves and the pistils? How does the slender stalk of the rose agree with the bulky head under which it bends? but the rose is a beautiful flower; and can we undertake to say that it does not owe a great deal of its beauty even to that disproportion; the rose is a large flower, yet it grows upon a small shrub; the flower of the apple is very small, and grows upon a large tree; yet the rose and the apple blossom are both beautiful, and the plants that bear them are most engagingly attired, notwithstanding this disproportion. What by general consent is allowed to be a more beautiful object than an orange-tree, nourishing at once with its leaves, its blossoms, and its fruit? but it is in vain that we search here for any proportion between the height, the breadth, or anything else concerning the dimensions of the whole, or concerning the relation of the particular parts to each other. I grant that we may observe in many flowers something of a regular figure, and of a methodical disposition of the leaves. The rose has such a figure and such a disposition of its petals; but in an oblique view, when this figure is in a good measure lost, and the order of the leaves confounded, it yet retains its beauty; the rose is even more beautiful before it is full blown; in the bud; before this exact figure is formed; and this is not the only instance wherein method and exactness, the soul of proportion, are found rather prejudicial than serviceable to the cause of beauty.

Section 3

PROPORTION NOT THE CAUSE OF
BEAUTY IN ANIMALS

That proportion has but a small share in the formation of beauty is full as evident among animals. Here the greatest variety of shapes and dispositions of parts are well fitted to excite this idea. The swan, confessedly a beautiful bird, has a neck longer than the rest of his body, and but a very short tail: is this a beautiful proportion? We must allow that it is. But then what shall we say to the peacock, who has comparatively but a short neck, with a tail longer than the neck and the rest of the body taken together? How many birds are there that vary infinitely from each of these standards, and from every other which you can fix; with proportions different, and often directly opposite to each other! and yet many of these birds are extremely beautiful; when upon considering them we find nothing in any one part that might determine us, *à priori*, to say what the others ought to be, nor indeed to guess anything about them, but what experience might show to be full of disappointment and mistake. And with regard to the colors either of birds or flowers, for there is something similar in the coloring of both, whether they are considered in their extension or gradation, there is nothing of proportion to be observed. Some are of but one single color; others have all the colors of the rainbow; some are of the primary colors, others are of the mixed; in short, an attentive observer may soon conclude that there is as little of proportion in the coloring as in the shapes of these objects. Turn next to beasts; examine the head of a beautiful horse; find what proportion that bears to his body, and to his limbs, and what relation these have to each other; and when you have settled these proportions as a standard of beauty, then take a dog or cat, or any other animal, and examine how far the same proportions between their heads and their necks, between those and the body, and so on, are found to hold; I think we may safely say, that they differ in every species, yet that there are individuals, found in a great many species so differing, that have a very striking beauty. Now, if it be allowed that very different, and even contrary forms and dispositions are consistent with beauty, it amounts I believe to a concession, that no certain measures, operating from a natural principle, are necessary to produce it; at least so far as the brute species is concerned.

Proportion Not the Cause of Beauty in the Human Species

There are some parts of the human body that are observed to hold certain proportions to each other; but before it can be proved that the efficient cause of beauty lies in these, it must be shown that, wherever these are found exact, the person to whom they belong is beautiful: I mean in the effect produced on the view, either of any member distinctly considered, or of the whole body together. It must be likewise shown, that these parts stand in such a relation to each other, that the comparison between them may be easily made, and that the affection of the mind may naturally result from it. For my part, I have at several times very carefully examined many of those proportions, and found them hold very nearly, or altogether alike in many subjects, which were not only very different from one another, but where one has been very beautiful, and the other very remote from beauty. With regard to the parts which are found so proportioned, they are often so remote from each other, in situation, nature, and office, that I cannot see how they admit of any comparison, nor consequently how any effect owing to proportion can result from them. The neck, say they, in beautiful bodies, should measure with the calf of the leg; it should likewise be twice the circumference of the wrist. And an infinity of observations of this kind are to be found in the writings and conversations of many. But what relation has the calf of the leg to the neck; or either of these parts to the wrist? These proportions are certainly to be found in handsome bodies. They are as certainly in ugly ones; as any who will take the pains to try may find. Nay, I do not know but they may be least perfect in some of the most beautiful. You may assign any proportions you please to every part of the human body; and I undertake that a painter shall religiously observe them all, and notwithstanding produce, if he pleases, a very ugly figure. The same painter shall considerably deviate from these proportions, and produce a very beautiful one. And, indeed, it may be observed in the masterpieces of the ancient and modern statuary, that several of them differ very widely from the proportions of others, in parts very conspicuous and of great consideration; and that they differ no less from the proportions we find in living men, of forms extremely striking and agreeable. And after all, how are the partisans of proportional beauty agreed amongst themselves about the proportions of the human body? Some hold it to be seven heads; some make it eight; whilst others extend it even to ten: a vast difference in such a small number of divisions! Others take other methods of estimating the proportions, and all with equal success. But are these proportions exactly the same in all handsome men? or are they at all the proportions found in beautiful women? Nobody will say that they are; yet both sexes are undoubtedly capable of beauty, and the female of the greatest; which advantage I believe will hardly be attributed to the superior exactness of proportion in the fair sex. Let us rest a moment on this point; and consider how much difference there is between the measures that prevail in many similar parts of the body, in the two sexes of this single species only. If you assign any determinate proportions to the limbs of a man, and if you limit human beauty to these proportions, when you find a woman who differs in the make and measures of almost every part, you must conclude her not to be beautiful, in spite of the suggestions of your imagination; or, in obedience to your imagination, you must renounce your rules; you must lay by the scale and compass, and look out for some other cause of beauty. For if beauty be attached to certain measures which operate from a *principle in nature*, why should similar parts with different measures of proportion be found to have beauty, and this too in the very same species? But to open our view a little, it is worth observing, that almost all animals have parts of very much the same nature, and destined nearly to the same purposes; a head, neck, body, feet, eyes, ears, nose, and mouth; yet Providence, to provide in the best manner for their several wants, and to display the riches of his wisdom and goodness in his creation, has worked out of these few and similar organs, and members, a diversity hardly short of infinite in their disposition, measures and relation. But, as we have before observed, amidst this infinite diversity, one particular is common to many species: several of the individuals which compose them are capable of affecting us with a sense of loveliness: and whilst they agree in producing this effect, they differ extremely in the relative measures of those parts which have produced it. These considerations were sufficient to induce me to reject the notion of any particular proportions that operated by nature to produce a pleasing effect; but those who will agree with me with regard to a particular proportion, are strongly prepossessed in favor of one more indefinite. They imagine, that although beauty in general is annexed to no certain measures common to the several kinds of pleasing plants and animals; yet that there is a certain proportion in each species absolutely essential to the beauty of that particular kind. If we consider the animal world in general, we find beauty confined to no certain measures; but as some peculiar measure and relation of parts is what distinguishes each peculiar class of animals, it must of necessity be, that the beautiful in each kind will be found in the measures and proportions of that kind; for otherwise it would deviate from its proper species, and become in some sort monstrous: however, no species is so strictly confined to any certain proportions, that there is not a considerable variation amongst the individuals; and as it has been shown of the human, so it may be shown of the brute kinds, that beauty is found indifferently in all the proportions which each kind can admit, without quitting its common form; and it is this idea of a common form that makes the proportion of parts at all regarded, and not the operation of any natural cause: indeed a little consideration will make it appear, that it is not measure, but manner, that creates all the beauty which belongs to shape. What light do we borrow from these boasted proportions, when we study ornamental design? It seems amazing to me, that artists, if they were as well convinced as they pretend to be, that proportion is a principal cause of beauty, have not by them at all times accurate measurements of all sorts of beautiful animals to help them to proper proportions, when they would contrive anything elegant; especially as they frequently assert that it is from an observation of the beautiful in nature they direct their practice. I know that it has been said long since, and echoed backward and forward from one writer to another a thousand times, that the proportions of building have been taken from those of the human body. To make this forced analogy complete, they represent a man with his arms raised and extended at full length, and then describe a sort of square, as it is formed by passing lines along the extremities of this strange figure. But it appears very clearly to me that the human figure never supplied the architect with any of his ideas. For, in the first place, men are very rarely seen in this strained posture; it is not natural to them; neither is it at all becoming. Secondly, the view of the human figure so disposed, does not naturally suggest the idea of a square, but rather of a cross; as that large space be tween the arms and the ground must be filled with something before it can make anybody think of a square. Thirdly, several buildings are by no means of the form of that particular square, which are notwithstanding planned by the best

EDMUND BURKE

architects, and produce an effect altogether as good, and perhaps a better. And certainly nothing could he more unaccountably whimsical, than for an architect to model his performance by the human figure, since no two things can have less resemblance or analogy, than a man, and a house or temple: do we need to observe that their purposes are entirely different? What I am apt to suspect is this: that these analogies were devised to give a credit to the works of art, by showing a conformity between them and the noblest works in nature; not that the latter served at all to supply hints for the perfection of the former. And I am the more fully convinced, that the patrons of proportion have transferred their artificial ideas to nature, and not borrowed from thence the proportions they use in works of art; because in any discussion of this subject they always quit as soon as possible the open field of natural beauties, the animal and vegetable kingdoms, and fortify themselves within the artificial lines and angles of architecture. For there is in mankind an unfortunate propensity to make themselves, their views, and their works, the measure of excellence in everything whatsoever. Therefore having observed that their dwellings were most commodious and firm when they were thrown into regular figures, with parts answerable to each other; they transferred these ideas to their gardens; they turned their trees into pillars, pyramids, and obelisks; they formed their hedges into so many green walls, and fashioned their walks into squares, triangles, and other mathematical figures, with exactness and symmetry; and they thought, if they were not imitating, they were at least improving nature, and teaching her to know her business. But nature has at last escaped from their discipline and their fetters; and our gardens, if nothing else, declare, we begin to feel that mathematical ideas are not the true measures of beauty. And surely they are full as little so in the animal as the vegetable world. For is it not extraordinary, that in these fine descriptive pieces, these innumerable odes and elegies which are in the mouths of all the world, and many of which have been the entertainment of ages, that in these pieces which describe love with such a passionate energy, and represent its object in such an infinite variety of lights, not one word is said of proportion, if it be, what some insist it is, the principal component of beauty; whilst, at the same time, several other qualities are very frequently and warmly mentioned? But if proportion has not this power, it may appear odd how men came originally to be so prepossessed in its favor. It arose, I imagine, from the fondness I have just mentioned, which men bear so remarkably to their own works and notions; it arose from false reasonings on the effects of the customary figure of animals; it arose from the Platonic theory of fitness and aptitude. For which reason, in the next section, I shall consider the effects of custom in the figure of animals; and afterwards the idea of fitness: since if proportion does not operate by a natural power attending some measures, it must be either by custom, or the idea of utility; there is no other way.

Section 5

Proportion Further Considered

If I am not mistaken, a great deal of the prejudice in favor of proportion has arisen, not so much from the observation of any certain measures found in beautiful bodies, as from a wrong idea of the relation which deformity bears to beauty, to which it has been considered as the opposite; on this principle it was concluded that where the causes of deformity were removed, beauty must naturally and necessarily be introduced. This I believe is a mistake. For *deformity* is opposed not to beauty, but to the *complete common form*. If one of the legs of a man be found shorter than the other, the man is deformed; because there is something wanting to complete the whole idea we form of a man; and this has the same effect in natural faults, as maiming and mutilation produce from accidents. So if the back be humped, the man is deformed; because his back has an unusual figure, and what carries with it the idea of some disease or misfortune; So if a man's neck be considerably longer or shorter than usual, we say he is deformed in that part, because men are not commonly made in that manner. But surely every hour's experience may convince us that a man may have his legs of an equal length, and resembling each other in all respects, and his neck of a just size, and his back quite straight, without having at the same time the least perceivable beauty. Indeed beauty is so far from belonging to the idea of custom, that in reality what affects us in that manner is extremely rare and uncommon. The beautiful strikes us as much by its novelty as the deformed itself. It is thus in those species of animals with which we are acquainted; and if one of a new species were represented, we should by no means wait until custom had settled an idea of proportion, before we decided concerning its beauty or ugliness: which shows that the general idea of beauty can be no more owing to customary than to natural proportion. Deformity arises from the want of the common proportions; but the necessary result of their existence in any object is not beauty. If we suppose proportion in natural things to be relative to custom and use, the nature of use and custom will show that beauty, which is a *positive* and powerful quality, cannot result from it. We are so wonderfully formed, that, whilst we are creatures vehemently desirous of novelty, we are as strongly attached to habit and custom. But it is the nature of things which hold us by custom, to affect us very little whilst we are in possession of them, but strongly when they are absent. I remember to have frequented a certain place, every day for a long time together; and I may truly say that, so far from finding pleasure in it, I was affected with a sort of weariness and disgust; I came, I went, I returned, without pleasure; yet if by any means I passed by the usual time of my going thither, I was remarkably uneasy, and was not quiet till I had got into my old track. They who use snuff, take it almost without being sensible that they take it, and the acute sense of smell is deadened, so as to feel hardly anything from so sharp a stimulus; yet deprive the snuff-taker of his box, and he is the most uneasy mortal in the world. Indeed so far are use and habit from being causes of pleasure merely as such, that the effect of constant use is to make all things of whatever kind entirely unaffecting. For as use at last takes off the painful effect of many things, it reduces the pleasurable effect in others in the same manner, and brings both to a sort of mediocrity and indifference. Very justly is use called a second nature; and our natural and common state is one of absolute indifference, equally prepared for pain or pleasure. But when we are thrown out of this state, or deprived of anything requisite to maintain us in it; when this chance does not happen by pleasure from some mechanical cause, we are always hurt. It is so with the second nature, custom, in all things which relate to it. Thus the want of the usual proportions in men and other animals is sure to disgust, though their presence is by no means any cause of real pleasure. It is true that the proportions laid down as causes of beauty in the human body, are frequently found in beautiful ones, because they are generally found in all mankind; but if it can be shown too that they are found without beauty, and that beauty frequently exists without them, and that this beauty, where it exists, always can be assigned to other less equivocal causes, it will naturally lead us to conclude that proportion and beauty are not ideas of the same nature. The true opposite to beauty is not disproportion or deformity, but *ugliness*: and as it proceeds from causes opposite to those of positive beauty, we cannot consider it until we come to treat of that. Between beauty and ugliness there is a sort of mediocrity, in which the assigned proportions are most commonly found; but this has no effect upon the passions.

Section 6

Fitness Not the Cause of Beauty

It is said that the idea of utility, or of a part's being well adapted to answer its end, is the cause of beauty, or indeed beauty itself. If it were not for this opinion, it had been impossible for the doctrine of proportion to have held its ground very long; the world would be soon weary of hearing of measures which related to nothing, either of a natural principle, or of a fitness to answer some end; the idea which mankind most commonly conceive of proportion, is the suitableness of means to certain ends, and, where this is not the question, very seldom trouble themselves about the effect of different measures of things. Therefore it was necessary for this theory to insist that not only artificial, but natural objects took their beauty from the fitness of the parts for their several purposes. But in framing this theory, I am apprehensive that experience was not sufficiently consulted. For, on that principle, the wedge-like snout of a swine, with its tough cartilage at the end, the little sunk eyes, and the whole make of the head, so well adapted to its offices of digging and rooting, would be extremely beautiful. The great bag hanging to the bill of a pelican, a thing highly useful to this animal, would be likewise as beautiful in our eyes. The hedge-hog, so well secured against all assaults by his prickly hide, and the porcupine with his missile quills, would be then considered as creatures of no small elegance. There are few animals whose parts are better contrived than those of a monkey: he has the hands of a man, joined to the springy limbs of a beast; he is admirably calculated for running, leaping, grappling, and climbing; and yet there are few animals which seem to have less beauty in the eyes of all mankind. I need say little on the trunk of the elephant, of such various usefulness, and which is so far from contributing to his beauty. How well fitted is the wolf for running and leaping! how admirably is the lion armed for battle! but will any one therefore call the elephant, the wolf, and the lion, beautiful animals? I believe nobody will think the form of a man's leg so well adapted to running, as those of a horse, a dog, a deer, and several other creatures; at least they have not that appearance: yet, I believe, a well-fashioned human leg will be allowed to far exceed all these in beauty. If the fitness of parts was what constituted the loveliness of their form, the actual employment of them would undoubtedly much augment it; but this, though it is sometimes so upon another principle, is far from being always the case. A bird on the wing is not so beautiful as when it is perched; nay, there are several of the domestic fowls which are seldom seen to fly, and which are nothing the less beautiful on that account; yet birds are so extremely different in their form from the beast and human kinds, that you cannot, on the principle of fitness, allow them anything agreeable, but in consideration of their parts being designed for quite other purposes. I never in my life chanced to see a peacock fly; and yet before, very long before I considered any aptitude in his form for the aërial life, I was struck with the extreme beauty which raises that bird above many of the best flying fowls in the world; though, for anything I saw, his way of living was much like that of the swine, which fed in the farm-yard along with him. The same may be said of cocks, hens, and the like; they are of the flying kind in figure; in their manner of moving not very different from men and beasts. To leave these foreign examples; if beauty in our own species was annexed to use, men would be much more lovely than women; and strength and agility would be considered as the only beauties. But to call strength by the name of beauty, to have but one denomination for the qualities of a Venus and Hercules, so totally different in almost all respects, is surely a strange confusion of ideas, or abuse of words. The cause of this confusion, I imagine, proceeds from our frequently perceiving the parts of the human and other animal bodies to be at once very beautiful, and very well adapted to their purposes; and we are deceived by a sophism, which makes us take that for a cause which is only a concomitant: this is the sophism of the fly; who imagined he raised a great dust, because he stood upon the chariot that really raised it. The stomach, the lungs, the liver, as well as other parts, are incomparably well adapted to their purposes; yet they are far from having any beauty. Again, many things are very beautiful, in which it is impossible to discern any idea of use. And I appeal to the first and most natural feelings of mankind, whether on beholding a beautiful eye, or a well-fashioned mouth, or a well-turned leg, any ideas of their being well fitted for seeing, eating, or running, ever present themselves. What idea of use is it that flowers excite, the most beautiful part of the vegetable world? It is true that the infinitely wise and good Creator has, of his bounty, frequently joined beauty to those things which he has made useful to us; but this does not prove that an idea of use and beauty are the same thing, or that they are any way dependent on each other.

Section 7

THE REAL EFFECTS OF FITNESS

When I excluded proportion and fitness from any share in beauty, I did not by any means intend to say that they were of no value, or that they ought to be disregarded in works of art. Works of art are the proper sphere of their power; and here it is that they have their full effect. Whenever the wisdom of our Creator intended that we should be affected with anything, he did not confide the execution of his design to the languid and precarious operation of our reason; but he endued it with powers and properties that prevent the understanding, and even the will; which, seizing upon the senses and imagination, captivate the soul, before the understanding is ready either to join with them, or to oppose them. It is by a long deduction, and much study, that we discover the adorable wisdom of God in his works: when we discover it the effect is very different, not only in the manner of acquiring it, but in its own nature, from that which strikes us without any preparation from the sublime or the beautiful. How different is the satisfaction of an anatomist, who discovers the use of the muscles and of the skin, the excellent contrivance of the one for the various movements of the body, and the wonderful texture of the other, at once a general covering, and at once a general outlet as well as inlet; how different is this from the affection which possesses an ordinary man at the sight of a delicate, smooth skin, and all the other parts of beauty, which require no investigation to be perceived! In the former case, whilst we look up to the Maker with admiration and praise, the object which causes it may be odious and distasteful; the latter very often so touches us by its power on the imagination, that we examine but little into the artifice of its contrivance; and we have need of a strong effort of our reason to disentangle our minds from the allurements of the object, to a consideration of that wisdom which invented so powerful a machine. The effect of proportion and fitness, at least so far as they proceed from a mere consideration of the work itself, produce approbation, the acquiescence of the understanding, but not love, nor any passion of that species. When we examine the structure of a watch, when we come to know thoroughly the use of every part of it, satisfied as we are with the fitness of the whole, we are far enough from perceiving anything like beauty in the watch-work itself; but let us look on the case, the labor of some curious artist in engraving, with little or no idea of use, we shall have a much livelier idea of beauty than we ever could have had from the watch itself, though the masterpiece of Graham. In beauty, as I said, the effect is previous to any knowledge of the use; but to judge of proportion, we must know the end for which any work is designed. According to the end, the proportion varies. Thus there is one proportion of a tower, another of a house; one proportion of a gallery, another of a hall, another of a chamber. To judge of the proportions of these, you must be first acquainted with the purposes for which they were designed. Good sense and experience acting together, find out what is fit to be done in every work of art. We are rational creatures, and in all our works we ought to regard their end and purpose; the gratification of any passion, how innocent soever, ought only to be of secondary consideration. Herein is placed the real power of fitness and proportion; they operate on the understanding considering them, which *approves* the work and acquiesces in it. The passions, and the imagination which principally raises them, have here very little to do. When a room appears in its original nakedness, bare walls and a plain ceiling: let its proportion be ever so excellent, it pleases very little; a cold approbation is the utmost we can reach; a much worse proportioned room with elegant mouldings and fine festoons, glasses, and other merely ornamental furniture, will make the imagination revolt against the reason; it will please much more than the naked proportion of the first room, which the understanding has so much approved, as admirably fitted for its purposes. What I have here said and before concerning proportion, is by no means to persuade people absurdly to neglect the idea of use in the works of art. It is only to show that these excellent things, beauty and proportion, are not the same; not that they should either of them be disregarded.

Section 8

THE RECAPITULATION

On the whole; if such parts in human bodies as are found proportioned, were likewise constantly found beautiful, as they certainly are not; or if they were so situated, as that a pleasure might flow from the comparison, which they seldom are; or if any assignable proportions were found, either in plants or animals, which were always attended with beauty, which never was the case; or if, where parts were well adapted to their purposes, they were constantly beautiful, and when no use appeared, there was no beauty, which is contrary to all experience; we might conclude that beauty consisted in proportion or utility. But since, in all respects, the case is quite otherwise; we may be satisfied that beauty does not depend on these, let it owe its origin to what else it will.

Section 9

Perfection Not the Cause of Beauty

There is another notion current, pretty closely allied to the former; that *perfection* is the constituent cause of beauty. This opinion has been made to extend much further than to sensible objects. But in these, so far is perfection, considered as such, from being the cause of beauty; that this quality, where it is highest, in the female sex, almost always carries with it an idea of weakness and imperfection. Women are very sensible of this; for which reason they learn to lisp, to totter in their walk, to counterfeit weakness, and even sickness. In all this they are guided by nature. Beauty in distress is much the most affecting beauty. Blushing has little less power; and modesty in general, which is a tacit allowance of imperfection, is itself considered as an amiable quality, and certainly heightens every other that is so. I know it is in every body's mouth, that we ought to love perfection. This is to me a sufficient proof, that it is not the proper object of love. Who ever said we *ought* to love a fine woman, or even any of these beautiful animals which please us? Here to be affected, there is no need of the concurrence of our will.

Section 10

How Far the Idea of Beauty May Be Applied to the Qualities of the Mind

Nor is this remark in general less applicable to the qualities of the mind. Those virtues which cause admiration, and are of the sublimer kind, produce terror rather than love; such as fortitude, justice, wisdom, and the like. Never was any man amiable by force of these qualities. Those which engage our hearts, which impress us with a sense of loveliness, are the softer virtues; easiness of temper, compassion, kindness, and liberality; though certainly those latter are of less immediate and momentous concern to society, and of less dignity. But it is for that reason that they are so amiable. The great virtues turn principally on dangers, punishments, and troubles, and are exercised, rather in preventing the worst mischiefs, than in dispensing favors; and are therefore not lovely, though highly venerable. The subordinate turn on reliefs, gratifications, and indulgences; and are therefore more lovely, though inferior in dignity. Those persons who creep into the hearts of most people, who are chosen as the companions of their softer hours, and their reliefs from care and anxiety, are never persons of shining qualities or strong virtues. It is rather the soft green of the soul on which we rest our eyes, that are fatigued with beholding more glaring objects. It is worth observing how we feel ourselves affected in reading the characters of Cæsar and Cato, as they are so finely drawn and contrasted in Sallust. In one the *ignoscendo largiundo*; in the other, *nil largiundo*. In one, the *miseris perfugium*; in the other, *malis perniciem*. In the latter we have much to admire, much to reverence, and perhaps something to fear; we respect him, but we respect him at a distance. The former makes us familiar with him; we love him, and he leads us whither he pleases. To draw things closer to our first and most natural feelings, I will add a remark made upon reading this section by an ingenious friend. The authority of a father, so useful to our well-being, and so justly venerable upon all accounts, hinders us from having that entire love for him that we have for our mothers, where the parental authority is almost melted down into the mother's fondness and indulgence. But we generally have a great love for our grandfathers, in whom this authority is removed a degree from us, and where the weakness of age mellows it into something of a feminine partiality.

Section 11

How Far the Idea of Beauty May Be Applied to Virtue

From what has been said in the foregoing section, we may easily see how far the application of beauty to virtue may be made with propriety. The general application of this quality to virtue has a strong tendency to confound our ideas of things, and it has given rise to an infinite deal of whimsical theory; as the affixing the name of beauty to proportion, congruity, and perfection, as well as to qualities of things yet more remote from our natural ideas of it, and from one another, has tended to confound our ideas of beauty, and left us no standard or rule to judge by, that was not even more uncertain and fallacious than our own fancies. This loose and inaccurate manner of speaking has therefore misled us both in the theory of taste and of morals; and induced us to remove the science of our duties from their proper basis (our reason, our relations, and our necessities), to rest it upon, foundations altogether visionary and unsubstantial.

Section 12

The Real Cause of Beauty

Having endeavored to show what beauty is not, it remains that we should examine, at least with equal attention, in what it really consists. Beauty is a thing much too affecting not to depend upon some positive qualities. And since it is no creature of our reason, since it strikes us without any reference to use, and even where no use at all can be discerned, since the order and method of nature is generally very different from our measures and proportions, we must conclude that beauty is, for the greater part, some quality in bodies acting mechanically upon the human mind by the intervention of the senses. We ought, therefore, to consider attentively in what manner those sensible qualities are disposed, in such things as by experience we find beautiful, or which excite in us the passion of love, or some correspondent affection.

Section 13

BEAUTIFUL OBJECTS SMALL

The most obvious point that presents itself to us in examining any object is its extent or quantity. And what degree of extent prevails in bodies that are held beautiful, may be gathered from the usual manner of expression concerning it. I am told that, in most languages, the objects of love are spoken of under diminutive epithets. It is so in all the languages of which I have any knowledge. In Greek the *ion* and other diminutive terms are almost always the terms of affection and tenderness. These diminutives were commonly added by the Greeks to the names of persons with whom they conversed on terms of friendship and familiarity. Though the Romans were a people of less quick and delicate feelings, yet they naturally slid into the lessening termination upon the same occasions. Anciently, in the English language, the diminishing *ling* was added to the names of persons and things that were the objects of love. Some we retain still, as *darling* (or little dear), and a few others. But to this day, in ordinary conversation, it is usual to add the endearing name of *little* to everything we love; the French and Italians make use of these affectionate diminutives even more than we. In the animal creation, out of our own species, it is the small we are inclined to be fond of; little birds, and some of the smaller kinds of beasts. A great beautiful thing is a manner of expression scarcely ever used; but that of a great ugly thing is very common. There is a wide difference between admiration and love. The sublime, which is the cause of the former, always dwells on great objects, and terrible; the latter on small ones, and pleasing; we submit to what we admire, but we love what submits to us; in one case we are forced, in the other we are flattered, into compliance. In short, the ideas of the sublime and the beautiful stand on foundations so different, that it is hard, I had almost said impossible, to think of reconciling them in the same subject, without considerably lessening the effect of the one or the other upon the passions. So that, attending to their quantity, beautiful objects are comparatively small.

Section 14

Smoothness

The next property constantly observable in such objects is *smoothness*;[15] a quality so essential to beauty, that I do not now recollect anything beautiful that is not smooth. In trees and flowers, smooth leaves are beautiful; smooth slopes of earth in gardens; smooth streams in the landscape; smooth coats of birds and beasts in animal beauties; in fine women, smooth skins; and in several sorts of ornamental furniture, smooth and polished surfaces. A very considerable part of the effect of beauty is owing to this quality; indeed the most considerable. For, take any beautiful object, and give it a broken, and rugged surface; and, however well formed it may be in other respects, it pleases no longer. Whereas, let it want ever so many of the other constituents, if it wants not this, it becomes more pleasing than almost all the others without it. This seems to me so evident, that I am a good deal surprised that none who have handled the subject have made any mention of the quality of smoothness in the enumeration of those that go to the forming of beauty. For, indeed, any ruggedness, any sudden, projection, any sharp angle, is in the highest degree contrary to that idea.

---

15. Part IV. sect. 20.

Section 15

Gradual Variation

But as perfectly beautiful bodies are not composed of angular parts, so their parts never continue long in the same right line.[16] They vary their direction every moment, and they change under the eye by a deviation continually carrying on, but for whose beginning or end you will find it difficult to ascertain a point. The view of a beautiful bird will illustrate this observation. Here we see the head increasing insensibly to the middle, from whence it lessens gradually until it mixes with the neck; the neck loses itself in a larger swell, which continues to the middle of the body, when the whole decreases again to the tail; the tail takes a new direction, but it soon varies its new course, it blends again with the other parts, and the line is perpetually changing, above, below, upon every side. In this description I have before me the idea of a dove; it agrees very well with most of the conditions of beauty. It is smooth and downy; its parts are (to use that expression) melted into one another; you are presented with no sudden protuberance through the whole, and yet the whole is continually changing. Observe that part of a beautiful woman where she is perhaps the most beautiful, about the neck and breasts; the smoothness, the softness, the easy and insensible swell; the variety of the surface, which is never for the smallest space the same; the deceitful maze through which the unsteady eye slides giddily, without knowing where to fix, or whither it is carried. Is not this a demonstration of that change of surface, continual, and yet hardly perceptible at any point, which forms one of the great constituents of beauty? It gives me no small pleasure to find that I can strengthen my theory in this point by the opinion of the very ingenious Mr. Hogarth, whose idea of the line of beauty I take in general to be extremely just. But the idea of variation, without attending so accurately to the *manner* of the variation, has led him to consider angular figures as beautiful; these figures, it is true, vary greatly, yet they vary in a sudden and broken manner, and I do not find any natural object which is angular, and at the same time beautiful. Indeed, few natural objects are entirely angular.

---

16. Part IV. sect. 23.

EDMUND BURKE

But I think those which approach the most nearly to it are the ugliest. I must add, too, that so for as I could observe of nature, though the varied line is that alone in which complete beauty is found, yet there is no particular line which is always found in the most completely beautiful, and which is therefore beautiful in preference to all other lines. At least I never could observe it.

Section 16

DELICACY

An air of robustness and strength is very prejudicial to beauty. An appearance of *delicacy*, and even of fragility, is almost essential to it. Whoever examines the vegetable or animal creation will find this observation to be founded in nature. It is not the oak, the ash, or the elm, or any of the robust trees of the forest which we consider as beautiful; they are awful and majestic, they inspire a sort of reverence. It is the delicate myrtle, it is the orange, it is the almond, it is the jasmine, it is the vine which we look on as vegetable beauties. It is the flowery species, so remarkable for its weakness and momentary duration, that gives us the liveliest idea of beauty and elegance. Among animals, the greyhound is more beautiful than the mastiff, and the delicacy of a jennet, a barb, or an Arabian horse, is much more amiable than the strength and stability of some horses of war or carriage. I need here say little of the fair sex, where I believe the point will be easily allowed me. The beauty of women is considerably owing to their weakness or delicacy, and is even enhanced by their timidity, a quality of mind analogous to it. I would not here be understood to say, that weakness betraying very bad health has any share in beauty; but the ill effect of this is not because it is weakness, but because the ill state of health, which produces such weakness, alters the other conditions of beauty; the parts in such a case collapse, the bright color, the *lumen purpureum juventæ* is gone, and the fine variation is lost in wrinkles, sudden breaks, and right lines.

Section 17

Beauty in Color

As to the colors usually found in beautiful bodies, it may be somewhat difficult to ascertain them, because, in the several parts of nature, there is an infinite variety. However, even in this variety, we may mark out something on which to settle. First, the colors of beautiful bodies must not be dusky or muddy, but clean and fair. Secondly, they must not be of the strongest kind. Those which seem most appropriated to beauty, are the milder of every sort; light greens; soft blues; weak whites; pink reds; and violets. Thirdly, if the colors be strong and vivid, they are always diversified, and the object is never of one strong color; there are almost always such a number of them (as in variegated flowers) that the strength and glare of each is considerably abated. In a fine complexion there is not only some variety in the coloring, but the colors: neither the red nor the white are strong and glaring. Besides, they are mixed in such a manner, and with such gradations, that it is impossible to fix the bounds. On the same principle it is that the dubious color in the necks and tails of peacocks, and about the heads of drakes, is so very agreeable. In reality, the beauty both of shape and coloring are as nearly related as we can well suppose it possible for things of such different natures to be.

Section 18

RECAPITULATION

On the whole, the qualities of beauty, as they are merely sensible qualities, are the following: First, to be comparatively small. Secondly, to be smooth. Thirdly, to have a variety in the direction of the parts; but, fourthly, to have those parts not angular, but melted, as it were, into each other. Fifthly, to be of a delicate frame, without any remarkable appearance of strength. Sixthly, to have its colors clear and bright, but not very strong and glaring. Seventhly, or if it should have any glaring color, to have it diversified with others. These are, I believe, the properties on which beauty depends; properties that operate by nature, and are less liable to be altered by caprice, or confounded by a diversity of tastes, than any other.

Section 19

The Physiognomy

The *physiognomy* has a considerable share in beauty, especially in that of our own species. The manners give a certain determination to the countenance; which, being observed to correspond pretty regularly with them, is capable of joining the effect of certain agreeable qualities of the mind to those of the body. So that to form a finished human beauty, and to give it its full influence, the face must be expressive of such gentle and amiable qualities, as correspond with the softness, smoothness, and delicacy of the outward form.

The Eye

I have hitherto purposely omitted to speak of the *eye*, which has so great a share in the beauty of the animal creation, as it did not fall so easily under the foregoing heads, though in fact it is reducible to the same principles. I think, then, that the beauty of the eye consists, first, in its *clearness*; what *colored* eye shall please most, depends a good deal on particular fancies; but none are pleased with an eye whose water (to use that term) is dull and muddy.[17] We are pleased with the eye in this view, on the principle upon which we like diamonds, clear water, glass, and such like transparent substances. Secondly, the motion of the eye contributes to its beauty, by continually shifting its direction; but a slow and languid motion is more beautiful than a brisk one; the latter is enlivening; the former lovely. Thirdly, with regard to the union of the eye with the neighboring parts, it is to hold the same rule that is given of other beautiful ones; it is not to make a strong deviation from the line of the neighboring parts; nor to verge into any exact geometrical figure. Besides all this, the eye affects, as it is expressive of some qualities of the mind, and its principal power generally arises from this; so that what we have just said of the physiognomy is applicable here.

17. Part IV. sect. 25.

Section 21

Ugliness

It may perhaps appear like a sort of repetition of what we have before said, to insist here upon the nature of *ugliness*; as I imagine it to be in all respects the opposite to those qualities which we have laid down for the constituents of beauty. But though ugliness be the opposite to beauty, it is not the opposite to proportion and fitness. For it is possible that a thing may be very ugly with any proportions, and with a perfect fitness to any uses. Ugliness I imagine likewise to be consistent enough with an idea of the sublime. But I would by no means insinuate that ugliness of itself is a sublime idea, unless united with such qualities as excite a strong terror.

Section 22

Grace

Gracefulness is an idea not very different from beauty; it consists in much the same things. Gracefulness is an idea belonging to *posture* and *motion*. In both these, to be graceful, it is requisite that there be no appearance of difficulty; there is required a small inflection of the body; and a composure of the parts in such a manner, as not to incumber each other, not to appear divided by sharp and sudden angles. In this case, this roundness, this delicacy of attitude and motion, it is that all the magic of grace consists, and what is called its *je ne sçai quoi*; as will be obvious to any observer, who considers attentively the Venus de Medicis, the Antinous or any statue generally allowed to be graceful in a high degree.

Section 23

ELEGANCE AND SPECIOUSNESS

When any body is composed of parts smooth and polished, without pressing upon each other, without showing any ruggedness or confusion, and at the same time affecting some *regular shape*, I call it *elegant*. It is closely allied to the beautiful, differing from it only in this *regularity*; which, however, as it makes a very material difference in the affection produced, may very well constitute another species. Under this head I rank those delicate and regular works of art, that imitate no determinate object in nature, as elegant buildings, and pieces of furniture. When any object partakes of the above-mentioned qualities, or of those of beautiful bodies, and is withal of great dimensions, it is full as remote from the idea of mere beauty; I call *fine* or *specious*.

Section 24

THE BEAUTIFUL IN FEELING

The foregoing description of beauty, so far as it is taken in by the eye, may he greatly illustrated by describing the nature of objects, which produce a similar effect through the touch. This I call the beautiful in *feeling*. It corresponds wonderfully with what causes the same species of pleasure to the sight. There is a chain in all our sensations; they are all but different sorts of feelings calculated to be affected by various sorts of objects, but all to be affected after the same manner. All bodies that are pleasant to the touch, are so by the slightness of the resistance they make. Resistance is either to motion along the surface, or to the pressure of the parts on one another: if the former be slight, we call the body smooth; if the latter, soft. The chief pleasure we receive by feeling, is in the one or the other of these qualities; and if there be a combination of both, our pleasure is greatly increased. This is so plain, that it is rather more fit to illustrate other things, than to be illustrated itself by an example. The next source of pleasure in this sense, as in every other, is the continually presenting somewhat new; and we find that bodies which continually vary their surface, are much the most pleasant or beautiful to the feeling, as any one that pleases may experience. The third property in such objects is, that though the surface continually varies its direction, it never varies it suddenly. The application of anything sudden, even though the impression itself have little or nothing of violence, is disagreeable. The quick application of a finger a little warmer or colder than usual, without notice, makes us start; a slight tap on the shoulder, not expected, has the same effect. Hence it is that angular bodies, bodies that suddenly vary the direction of the outline, afford so little pleasure to the feeling. Every such change is a sort of climbing or falling in miniature; so that squares, triangles, and other angular figures are neither beautiful to the sight nor feeling. Whoever compares his state of mind, on feeling soft, smooth, variated, unangular bodies, with that in which he finds himself, on the view of a beautiful object, will perceive a very striking analogy in the effects of both; and which may go a good way towards discovering their common cause. Feeling and sight, in this respect, differ in but a few points. The touch takes in the pleasure of softness, which is not primarily an object of sight; the sight, on the other hand, comprehends color, which can hardly he made perceptible to the touch: the touch, again, has the advantage in a new idea of pleasure resulting from a moderate degree of warmth; but the eye triumphs in the infinite extent and multiplicity of its objects. But there is such a similitude in the pleasures of these senses, that I am apt to fancy, if it were possible that one might discern color by feeling (as it is said some blind men have done) that the same colors, and the same disposition of coloring, which are found beautiful to the sight, would be found likewise most grateful to the touch. But, setting aside conjectures, let us pass to the other sense; of hearing.

The Beautiful in Sounds

In this sense we find an equal aptitude to be affected in a soft and delicate manner; and how far sweet or beautiful sounds agree with our descriptions of beauty in other senses, the experience of every one must decide. Milton has described this species of music in one of his juvenile poems.[18] I need not say that Milton was perfectly well versed in that art; and that no man had a finer ear, with a happier manner of expressing the affections of one sense by metaphors taken from another. The description is as follows:—

> *"And ever against eating cares,*
> *Lap me in* soft *Lydian airs;*
> *In notes with many a* winding *bout*
> *Of* linked sweetness long drawn *out;*
> *With wanton heed, and giddy cunning,*
> *The* melting *voice through* mazes *running;*
> Untwisting *all the chains that tie*
> *The hidden soul of harmony."*

Let us parallel this with the softness, the winding surface, the unbroken continuance, the easy gradation of the beautiful in other things; and all the diversities of the several senses, with all their several affections, will rather help to throw lights from one another to finish one clear, consistent idea of the whole, than to obscure it by their intricacy and variety.

To the above-mentioned description I shall add one or two remarks. The first is; that the beautiful in music will not bear that loudness and strength of sounds, which may be used to raise other passions; nor notes which are shrill, or harsh, or deep; it agrees best with such as are clear, even, smooth, and weak. The second is; that great variety, and quick transitions from one measure or tone to another, are contrary to the

---

18. L'Allegro.

genius of the beautiful in music. Such[19] transitions often excite mirth, or other sudden or tumultuous passions; but not that sinking, that melting, that languor, which is the characteristical effect of the beautiful as it regards every sense. The passion excited by beauty is in fact nearer to a species of melancholy, than to jollity and mirth. I do not here mean to confine music to any one species of notes, or tones, neither is it an art in which I can say I have any great skill. My sole design in this remark is to settle a consistent idea of beauty. The infinite variety of the affections of the soul will suggest to a good head, and skilful ear, a variety of such sounds as are fitted to raise them. It can be no prejudice to this, to clear and distinguish some few particulars that belong to the same class, and are consistent with each other, from the immense crowd of different and sometimes contradictory ideas, that rank vulgarly under the standard of beauty. And of these it is my intention to mark such only of the leading points as show the conformity of the sense of hearing with all the other senses, in the article of their pleasures.

19. *"I ne'er am merry, when I hear sweet music."* —SHAKESPEARE.

Taste and Smell

This general agreement of the senses is yet more evident on minutely considering those of taste and smell. We metaphorically apply the idea of sweetness to sights and sounds; but as the qualities of bodies by which they are fitted to excite either pleasure or pain in these senses are not so obvious as they are in the others, we shall refer an explanation of their analogy, which is a very close one, to that part wherein we come to consider the common efficient cause of beauty, as it regards all the senses. I do not think anything better fitted to establish a clear and settled idea of visual beauty than this way of examining the similar pleasures of other senses; for one part is sometimes clear in one of the senses that is more obscure in another; and where there is a clear concurrence of all, we may with more certainty speak of any one of them. By this means, they bear witness to each other; nature is, as it were, scrutinized; and we report nothing of her but what we receive from her own information.

Section 27

THE SUBLIME AND BEAUTIFUL COMPARED

On closing this general view of beauty, it naturally occurs that we should compare it with the sublime; and in this comparison there appears a remarkable contrast. For sublime objects are vast in their dimensions, beautiful ones comparatively small; beauty should be smooth and polished; the great, rugged and negligent: beauty should shun the right line, yet deviate from it insensibly; the great in many cases loves the right line; and when it deviates, it often makes a strong deviation: beauty should not be obscure; the great ought to be dark and gloomy: beauty should be light and delicate; the great ought to be solid, and even massive. They are indeed ideas of a very different nature, one being founded on pain, the other on pleasure; and, however they may vary afterwards from the direct nature of their causes, yet these causes keep up an eternal distinction between them, a distinction never to be forgotten by any whose business it is to affect the passions. In the infinite variety of natural combinations, we must expect to find the qualities of things the most remote imaginable from each other united in the same object. We must expect also to find combinations of the same kind in the works of art. But when we consider the power of an object upon our passions, we must know that when anything is intended to affect the mind by the force of some predominant property, the affection produced is like to be the more uniform and perfect, if all the other properties or qualities of the object be of the same nature, and tending to the same design as the principal.

> *"If black and white blend, soften, and unite*
> *A thousand ways, are there no black and white?"*

If the qualities of the sublime and beautiful are sometimes found united, does this prove that they are the same; does it prove that they are any way allied; does it prove even that they are not opposite and contradictory? Black and white may soften, may blend; but they are not therefore the same. Nor, when they are so softened and blended with each other, or with different colors, is the power of black as black, or of white as white, so strong as when each stands uniform and distinguished.

PART 4

Section 1

OF THE EFFICIENT CAUSE OF THE SUBLIME AND BEAUTIFUL

When I say, I intend to inquire into the efficient cause of sublimity and beauty, I would not be understood to say, that I can come to the ultimate cause. I do not pretend that I shall ever be able to explain why certain affections of the body produce such a distinct emotion of mind, and no other; or why the body is at all affected by the mind, or the mind by the body. A little thought will show this to be impossible. But I conceive, if we can discover what affections of the mind produce certain emotions of the body; and what distinct feelings and qualities of body shall produce certain determinate passions in the mind, and no others, I fancy a great deal will be done; something not unuseful towards a distinct knowledge of our passions, so far at least as we have them at present under our consideration. This is all, I believe, we can do. If we could advance a step farther, difficulties would still remain, as we should be still equally distant from the first cause. When Newton first discovered the property of attraction, and settled its laws, he found it served very well to explain several of the most remarkable phenomena in nature; but yet, with reference to the general system of things, he could consider attraction but as an effect, whose cause at that time he did not attempt to trace. But when he afterwards began to account for it by a subtle elastic ether, this great man (if in so great a man it be not impious to discover anything like a blemish) seemed to have quitted his usual cautious manner of philosophizing; since, perhaps, allowing all that has been advanced on this subject to be sufficiently proved, I think it leaves us with as many difficulties as it found us. That great chain of causes, which, linking one to another, even to the throne of God himself, can never be unravelled by any industry of ours. When we go but one step beyond the immediate sensible qualities of things, we go out of our depth. All we do after is but a faint struggle, that shows we are in an element which does not belong to us. So that when I speak of cause, and efficient cause, I only mean certain affections of the mind, that cause certain changes in the body; or certain powers and properties in bodies, that work a change in the mind. As, if I were to explain the motion of a body falling to the ground, I would say it was caused by gravity; and I would endeavor to show after what manner this power operated, without attempting to show why it operated in this manner: or, if I were to explain the effects of bodies striking one another by the common laws of percussion, I should not endeavor to explain how motion itself is communicated.

Section 2

ASSOCIATION

I t is no small bar in the way of our inquiry into the cause of our passions, that the occasions of many of them are given, and that their governing motions are communicated at a time when we have not capacity to reflect on them; at a time of which all sort of memory is worn out of our minds. For besides such things as affect us in various manners, according to their natural powers, there are associations made at that early season, which we find it very hard afterwards to distinguish from natural effects. Not to mention the unaccountable antipathies which we find in many persons, we all find it impossible to remember when a steep became more terrible than a plain; or fire or water more terrible than a clod of earth; though all these are very probably either conclusions from experience, or arising from the premonitions of others; and some of them impressed, in all likelihood, pretty late. But as it must be allowed that many things affect us after a certain manner, not by any natural powers they have for that purpose, but by association; so it would be absurd, on the other hand, to say that all things affect us by association only; since some things must have been originally and naturally agreeable or disagreeable, from which the others derive their associated powers; and it would be, I fancy, to little purpose to look for the cause of our passions in association, until we fail of it in the natural properties of things.

Section 3

CAUSE OF PAIN AND FEAR

I have before observed,[20] that whatever is qualified to cause terror is a foundation capable of the sublime; to which I add, that not only these, but many things from which we cannot probably apprehend any danger, have a similar effect, because they operate in a similar manner. I observed, too,[21] that whatever produces pleasure, positive and original pleasure, is fit to have beauty engrafted on it. Therefore, to clear up the nature of these qualities, it may be necessary to explain the nature of pain and pleasure on which they depend. A man who suffers under violent bodily pain, (I suppose the most violent, because the effect may be the more obvious,) I say a man in great pain has his teeth set, his eyebrows are violently contracted, his forehead is wrinkled, his eyes are dragged inwards, and rolled with great vehemence, his hair stands on end, the voice is forced out in short shrieks and groans, and the whole fabric totters. Fear or terror, which is an apprehension of pain or death, exhibits exactly the same effects, approaching in violence to those just mentioned, in proportion to the nearness of the cause, and the weakness of the subject. This is not only so in the human species: but I have more than once observed in dogs, under an apprehension of punishment, that they have writhed their bodies, and yelped, and howled, as if they had actually felt the blows. From hence I conclude, that pain and fear act upon the same parts of the body, and in the same manner, though somewhat differing in degree: that pain and fear consist in an unnatural tension of the nerves; that this is sometimes accompanied with an unnatural strength, which sometimes suddenly changes into an extraordinary weakness; that these effects often come on alternately, and are sometimes mixed with each other. This is the nature of all convulsive agitations, especially in weaker subjects, which are the most liable to the severest impressions of pain and fear. The only difference between pain and terror is, that things which cause pain operate on the mind by the intervention of the body; whereas things

---

20. Part I. sect. 7.
21. Part I. sect. 10.

EDMUND BURKE

that cause terror generally affect the bodily organs by the operation of the mind suggesting the danger; but both agreeing, either primarily or secondarily, in producing a tension, contraction, or violent emotion of the nerves,[22] they agree likewise in everything else. For it appears very clearly to me from this, as well as from many other examples, that when the body is disposed, by any means whatsoever, to such emotions as it would acquire by the means of a certain passion; it will of itself excite something very like that passion in the mind.

---

22. I do not here enter into the question debated among physiologists, whether pain be the effect of a contraction, or a tension of the nerves. Either will serve my purpose; for by tension, I mean no more than a violent pulling of the fibres which compose any muscle or membrane, in whatever way this is done.

Section 4

Continued

To this purpose Mr. Spon, in his "Récherches d'Antiquité," gives us a curious story of the celebrated physiognomist Campanella. This man, it seems, had not only made very accurate observations on human faces, but was very expert in mimicking such as were any way remarkable. When he had a mind to penetrate into the inclinations of those he had to deal with, he composed his face, his gesture, and his whole body, as nearly as he could into the exact similitude of the person he intended to examine; and then carefully observed what turn of mind he seemed to acquire by this change. So that, says my author, he was able to enter into the dispositions and thoughts of people as effectually as if he had been changed into the very men. I have often observed, that on mimicking the looks and gestures of angry, or placid, or frighted, or daring men, I have involuntarily found my mind turned to that passion, whose appearance I endeavored to imitate; nay, I am convinced it is hard to avoid it, though one strove to separate the passion from its correspondent gestures. Our minds and bodies are so closely and intimately connected, that one is incapable of pain or pleasure without the other. Campanella, of whom we have been speaking, could so abstract his attention from any sufferings of his body, that he was able to endure the rack itself without much pain; and in lesser pains everybody must have observed that, when we can employ our attention on anything else, the pain has been for a time suspended: on the other hand, if by any means the body is indisposed to perform such gestures, or to be stimulated into such emotions as any passion usually produces in it, that passion itself never can arise, though its cause should be never so strongly in action; though it should be merely mental, and immediately affecting none of the senses. As an opiate, or spirituous liquors, shall suspend the operation of grief, or fear, or anger, in spite of all our efforts to the contrary; and this by inducing in the body a disposition contrary to that which it receives from these passions.

Section 5

HOW THE SUBLIME IS PRODUCED

Having considered terror as producing an unnatural tension and certain violent emotions of the nerves; it easily follows, from what we have just said, that whatever is fitted to produce such a tension must be productive of a passion similar to terror,[23] and consequently must be a source of the sublime, though it should have no idea of danger connected with it. So that little remains towards showing the cause of the sublime, but to show that the instances we have given of it in the second part relate to such things, as are fitted by nature to produce this sort of tension, either by the primary operation of the mind or the body. With regard to such things as affect by the associated idea of danger, there can be no doubt but that they produce terror, and act by some modification of that passion; and that terror, when sufficiently violent, raises the emotions of the body just mentioned, can as little be doubted. But if the sublime is built on terror or some passion like it, which has pain for its object, it is previously proper to inquire how any species of delight can be derived from a cause so apparently contrary to it. I say *delight*, because, as I have often remarked, it is very evidently different in its cause, and in its own nature, from actual and positive pleasure.

---

23. Part II. sect. 2.

Section 6

How Pain Can Be a Cause of Delight

Providence has so ordered it, that a state of rest and inaction, however it may flatter our indolence, should be productive of many inconveniences; that it should generate such disorders, as may force us to have recourse to some labor, as a thing absolutely requisite to make us pass our lives with tolerable satisfaction; for the nature of rest is to suffer all the parts of our bodies to fall into a relaxation, that not only disables the members from performing their functions, but takes away the vigorous tone of fibre which is requisite for carrying on the natural and necessary secretions. At the same time, that in this languid in active state, the nerves are more liable to the most horrid convulsions, than when they are sufficiently braced and strengthened. Melancholy, dejection, despair, and often self-murder, is the consequence of the gloomy view we take of things in this relaxed state of body. The best remedy for all these evils is exercise or *labor*; and labor is a surmounting of *difficulties*, an exertion of the contracting power of the muscles; and as such resembles pain, which consists in tension or contraction, in everything but degree. Labor is not only requisite to preserve the coarser organs, in a state fit for their functions; but it is equally necessary to these finer and more delicate organs, on which, and by which, the imagination and perhaps the other mental powers act. Since it is probable, that not only the inferior parts of the soul, as the passions are called, but the understanding itself makes use of some fine corporeal instruments in its operation; though what they are, and where they are, may be somewhat hard to settle: but that it does make use of such, appears from hence; that a long exercise of the mental powers induces a remarkable lassitude of the whole body; and on the other hand, that great bodily labor, or pain, weakens and sometimes actually destroys the mental faculties. Now, as a due exercise is essential to the coarse muscular parts of the constitution, and that without this rousing they would become languid and diseased, the very same rule holds with regard to those finer parts we have mentioned; to have them in proper order, they must be shaken and worked to a proper degree.

EDMUND BURKE

Section 7

EXERCISE NECESSARY FOR THE FINER ORGANS

As common labor, which is a mode of pain, is the exercise of the grosser, a mode of terror is the exercise of the finer parts of the system; and if a certain mode of pain be of such a nature as to act upon the eye or the ear, as they are the most delicate organs, the affection approaches more nearly to that which has a mental cause. In all these cases, if the pain and terror are so modified as not to be actually noxious; if the pain is not carried to violence, and the terror is not conversant about the present destruction of the person, as these emotions clear the parts, whether fine or gross, of a dangerous and troublesome incumbrance, they are capable of producing delight; not pleasure, but a sort of delightful horror, a sort of tranquillity tinged with terror; which, as it belongs to self-preservation, is one of the strongest of all the passions. Its object is the sublime.[24] Its highest degree I call *astonishment*; the subordinate degrees are awe, reverence, and respect, which, by the very etymology of the words, show from what source they are derived, and how they stand distinguished from positive pleasure.

---

24. Part II. sect. 1.

Section 8

Why Things Not Dangerous Sometimes Produce a Passion Like Terror

A mode of terror or pain is always the cause of the sublime.[25] For terror or associated danger, the foregoing explication is, I believe, sufficient. It will require something more trouble to show, that such examples as I have given of the sublime in the second part are capable of producing a mode of pain, and of being thus allied to terror, and to be accounted for on the same principles. And first of such objects as are great in their dimensions. I speak of visual objects.

---

25. Part I. sect. 7. Part II. sect. 2.

Section 9

WHY VISUAL OBJECTS OF GREAT DIMENSIONS ARE SUBLIME

Vision is performed by having a picture, formed by the rays of light which are reflected from the object, painted in one piece, instantaneously, on the retina, or last nervous part of the eye. Or, according to others, there is but one point of any object painted on the eye in such a manner as to be perceived at once, but by moving the eye, we gather up, with great celerity, the several parts of the object, so as to form one uniform piece. If the former opinion be allowed, it will be considered,[26] that though all the light reflected from a large body should strike the eye in one instant; yet we must suppose that the body itself is formed of a vast number of distinct points, every one of which, or the ray from every one, makes an impression on the retina. So that, though the image of one point should cause but a small tension of this membrane, another, and another, and another stroke, must in their progress cause a very great one, until it arrives at last to the highest degree; and the whole capacity of the eye, vibrating in all its parts, must approach near to the nature of what causes pain, and consequently must produce an idea of the sublime. Again, if we take it, that one point only of an object is distinguishable at once; the matter will amount nearly to the same thing, or rather it will make the origin of the sublime from greatness of dimension yet clearer. For if but one point is observed at once, the eye must traverse the vast space of such bodies with great quickness, and consequently the fine nerves and muscles destined to the motion of that part must be very much strained; and their great sensibility must make them highly affected by this straining. Besides, it signifies just nothing to the effect produced, whether a body has its parts connected and makes its impression at once; or, making but one impression of a point at a time, it causes a succession of the same or others so quickly as to make them seem united; as is evident from the common effect of whirling about a lighted torch or piece of wood: which, if done with celerity, seems a circle of fire.

---

26. Part II. sect. 7.

Section 10

Unity Why Requisite to Vastness

It may be objected to this theory, that the eye generally receives an equal number of rays at all times, and that therefore a great object cannot affect it by the number of rays, more than that variety of objects which the eye must always discern whilst it remains open. But to this I answer, that admitting an equal number of rays, or an equal quantity of luminous particles to strike the eye at all times, yet if these rays frequently vary their nature, now to blue, now to red, and so on, or their manner of termination, as to a number of petty squares, triangles, or the like, at every change, whether of color or shape, the organ has a sort of relaxation or rest; but this relaxation and labor so often interrupted, is by no means productive of ease; neither has it the effect of vigorous and uniform labor. Whoever has remarked the different effects of some strong exercise, and some little piddling action, will understand why a teasing, fretful employment, which at once wearies and weakens the body, should have nothing great; these sorts of impulses, which are rather teasing than painful, by continually and suddenly altering their tenor and direction, prevent that full tension, that species of uniform labor, which is allied to strong pain, and causes the sublime. The sum total of things of various kinds, though it should equal the number of the uniform parts composing some *one* entire object, is not equal in its effect upon the organs of our bodies. Besides the one already assigned, there is another very strong reason for the difference. The mind in reality hardly ever can attend diligently to more than one thing at a time; if this thing be little, the effect is little, and a number of other little objects cannot engage the attention; the mind is bounded by the bounds of the object; and what is not attended to, and what does not exist, are much the same in the effect; but the eye or the mind, (for in this case there is no difference,) in great, uniform objects, does not readily arrive at their bounds; it has no rest, whilst it contemplates them; the image is much the same everywhere. So that everything great by its quantity must necessarily be one, simple and entire.

Section 11

THE ARTIFICIAL INFINITE

We have observed that a species of greatness arises from the artificial infinite; and that this infinite consists in an uniform succession of great parts: we observed too, that the same uniform succession had a like power in sounds. But because the effects of many things are clearer in one of the senses than in another, and that all the senses bear analogy to and illustrate one another, I shall begin with this power in sounds, as the cause of the sublimity from succession is rather more obvious in the sense of hearing. And I shall here, once for all, observe, that an investigation of the natural and mechanical causes of our passions, besides the curiosity of the subject, gives, if they are discovered, a double strength and lustre to any rules we deliver on such matters. When the ear receives any simple sound, it is struck by a single pulse of the air which makes the ear-drum and the other membranous parts vibrate according to the nature and species of the stroke. If the stroke be strong, the organ of hearing suffers a considerable degree of tension. If the stroke be repeated pretty soon after, the repetition causes an expectation of another stroke. And it must be observed, that expectation itself causes a tension. This is apparent in many animals, who, when they prepare for hearing any sound, rouse themselves, and prick up their ears; so that here the effect of the sounds is considerably augmented by a new auxiliary, the expectation. But though after a number of strokes, we expect still more, not being able to ascertain the exact time of their arrival, when they arrive, they produce a sort of surprise, which increases this tension yet further. For I have observed, that when at any time I have waited very earnestly for some sound, that returned at intervals, (as the successive firing of cannon,) though I fully expected the return of the sound, when it came it always made me start a little; the ear-drum suffered a convulsion, and the whole body consented with it. The tension of the part thus increasing at every blow, by the united forces of the stroke itself, the expectation and the surprise, it is worked up to such a pitch as to be capable of the sublime; it is brought just to the verge of pain. Even when the cause has ceased, the organs of hearing being often successively struck in a similar manner, continue to vibrate in that manner for some time longer; this is an additional help to the greatness of the effect.

The Vibrations Must Be Similar

But if the vibration be not similar at every impression, it can never be carried beyond the number of actual impressions; for, move any body as a pendulum, in one way, and it will continue to oscillate in an arch of the same circle, until the known causes make it rest; but if, after first putting it in motion in one direction, you push it into another, it can never reassume the first direction; because it can never move itself, and consequently it can have but the effect of that last motion; whereas, if in the same direction you act upon it several times, it will describe a greater arch, and move a longer time.

Section 13

THE EFFECTS OF SUCCESSION IN VISUAL OBJECTS EXPLAINED

If we can comprehend clearly how things operate upon one of our senses, there can be very little difficulty in conceiving in what manner they affect the rest. To say a great deal therefore upon the corresponding affections of every sense, would tend rather to fatigue us by an useless repetition, than to throw any new light upon the subject by that ample and diffuse manner of treating it; but as in this discourse we chiefly attach ourselves to the sublime, as it affects the eye, we shall consider particularly why a successive disposition of uniform parts in the same right line should be sublime,[27] and upon what principle this disposition is enabled to make a comparatively small quantity of matter produce a grander effect, than a much larger quantity disposed in another manner. To avoid the perplexity of general notions; let us set before our eyes, a colonnade of uniform pillars planted in a right line; let us take our stand in such a manner, that the eye may shoot along this colonnade, for it has its best effect in this view. In our present situation it is plain, that the rays from the first round pillar will cause in the eye a vibration of that species; an image of the pillar itself. The pillar immediately succeeding increases it; that which follows renews and enforces the impression; each in its order as it succeeds, repeats impulse after impulse, and stroke after stroke, until the eye, long exercised in one particular way, cannot lose that object immediately, and, being violently roused by this continued agitation, it presents the mind with a grand or sublime conception. But instead of viewing a rank of uniform pillars, let us suppose that they succeed each other, a round and a square one alternately. In this case the vibration caused by the first round pillar perishes as soon as it is formed; and one of quite another sort (the square) directly occupies its place; which however it resigns as quickly to the round one; and thus the eye proceeds, alternately, taking up one image, and laying down another, as long as the building continues. From whence it is obvious that, at the last pillar, the impression is as far from continuing as it was at the very

27. Part II. sect. 10.

first; because, in fact, the sensory can receive no distinct impression but from the last; and it can never of itself resume a dissimilar impression: besides every variation of the object is a rest and relaxation to the organs of sight; and these reliefs prevent that powerful emotion so necessary to produce the sublime. To produce therefore a perfect grandeur in such things as we have been mentioning, there should be a perfect simplicity, an absolute uniformity in disposition, shape, and coloring. Upon this principle of succession and uniformity it may be asked, why a long bare wall should not be a more sublime object than a colonnade; since the succession is no way interrupted; since the eye meets no check; since nothing more uniform can be conceived? A long bare wall is certainly not so grand an object as a colonnade of the same length and height. It is not altogether difficult to account for this difference. When we look at a naked wall, from the evenness of the object, the eye runs along its whole space, and arrives quickly at its termination; the eye meets nothing which may interrupt its progress; but then it meets nothing which may detain it a proper time to produce a very great and lasting effect. The view of a bare wall, if it be of a great height and length, is undoubtedly grand; but this is only *one* idea, and not a *repetition* of *similar* ideas: it is therefore great, not so much upon the principle of *infinity*, as upon that of *vastness*. But we are not so powerfully affected with any one impulse, unless it be one of a prodigious force indeed, as we are with a succession of similar impulses; because the nerves of the sensory do not (if I may use the expression) acquire a habit of repeating the same feeling in such a manner as to continue it longer than its cause is in action; besides, all the effects which I have attributed to expectation and surprise in Sect. 11, can have no place in a bare wall.

Section 14

LOCKE'S OPINION CONCERNING DARKNESS CONSIDERED

It is Mr. Locke's opinion, that darkness is not naturally an idea of terror; and that, though an excessive light is painful to the sense, the greatest excess of darkness is no ways troublesome. He observes indeed in another place, that a nurse or an old woman having once associated the ideas of ghosts and goblins with that of darkness, night, ever after, becomes painful and horrible to the imagination. The authority of this great man is doubtless as great as that of any man can be, and it seems to stand in the way of our general principle.[28] We have considered darkness as a cause of the sublime; and we have all along considered the sublime as depending on some modification of pain or terror: so that if darkness be no way painful or terrible to any, who have not had their minds early tainted with superstitions, it can be no source of the sublime to them. But, with all deference to such an authority, it seems to me, that an association of a more general nature, an association which takes in all mankind, may make darkness terrible; for in utter darkness it is impossible to know in what degree of safety we stand; we are ignorant of the objects that surround us; we may every moment strike against some dangerous obstruction; we may fall down a precipice the first step we take; and if an enemy approach, we know not in what quarter to defend ourselves; in such a case strength is no sure protection; wisdom can only act by guess; the boldest are staggered, and he who would pray for nothing else towards his defence is forced to pray for light.

As to the association of ghosts and goblins; surely it is more natural to think that darkness, being originally an idea of terror, was chosen as a fit scene for such terrible representations, than that such representations have made darkness terrible. The mind of man very easily slides into an error of the former sort; but it is very hard to imagine, that the effect of an idea so universally terrible in all times, and in all countries, as darkness, could possibly have been owing to a set of idle stories, or to any cause of a nature so trivial, and of an operation so precarious.

---

28. Part II. sect. 3.

DARKNESS TERRIBLE IN ITS OWN NATURE

Perhaps it may appear on inquiry, that blackness and darkness are in some degree painful by their natural operation, independent of any associations whatsoever. I must observe, that the ideas of darkness and blackness are much the same; and they differ only in this, that blackness is a more confined idea. Mr. Cheselden has given us a very curious story of a boy who had been born blind, and continued so until he was thirteen or fourteen years old; he was then couched for a cataract, by which operation he received his sight. Among many remarkable particulars that attended his first perceptions and judgments on visual objects, Cheselden tells us, that the first time the boy saw a black object, it gave him great uneasiness; and that some time after, upon accidentally seeing a negro woman, he was struck with great horror at the sight. The horror, in this case, can scarcely be supposed to arise from any association. The boy appears by the account to have been particularly observing and sensible for one of his age; and therefore it is probable, if the great uneasiness he felt at the first sight of black had arisen from its connection with any other disagreeable ideas, he would have observed and mentioned it. For an idea, disagreeable only by association, has the cause of its ill effect on the passions evident enough at the first impression; in ordinary cases, it is indeed frequently lost; but this is because the original association was made very early, and the consequent impression repeated often. In our instance, there was no time for such a habit; and there is no reason to think that the ill effects of black on his imagination were more owing to its connection with any disagreeable ideas, than that the good effects of more cheerful colors were derived from their connection with pleasing ones. They had both probably their effects from their natural operation.

Section 16

WHY DARKNESS IS TERRIBLE

It may be worth while to examine how darkness can operate in such a manner as to cause pain. It is observable, that still as we recede from the light, nature has so contrived it, that the pupil is enlarged by the retiring of the iris, in proportion to our recess. Now, instead of declining from it but a little, suppose that we withdraw entirely from the light; it is reasonable to think that the contraction of the radial fibres of the iris is proportionally greater; and that this part may by great darkness come to be so contracted, as to strain the nerves that compose it beyond their natural tone; and by this means to produce a painful sensation. Such a tension it seems there certainly is, whilst we are involved in darkness; for in such a state, whilst the eye remains open, there is a continual nisus to receive light; this is manifest from the flashes and luminous appearances which often seem in these circumstances to play before it; and which can be nothing but the effect of spasms, produced by its own efforts in pursuit of its object: several other strong impulses will produce the idea of light in the eye, besides the substance of light itself, as we experience on many occasions. Some, who allow darkness to be a cause of the sublime, would infer, from the dilatation of the pupil, that a relaxation may be productive of the sublime as well as a convulsion: but they do not, I believe, consider, that although the circular ring of the iris be in some sense a sphincter, which may possibly be dilated by a simple relaxation, yet in one respect it differs from most of the other sphincters of the body, that it is furnished with antagonist muscles, which are the radial fibres of the iris: no sooner does the circular muscle begin to relax, than these fibres, wanting their counterpoise, are forcibly drawn back, and open the pupil to a considerable wideness. But though we were not apprised of this, I believe any one will find, if he opens his eyes and makes an effort to see in a dark place, that a very perceivable pain ensues. And I have heard some ladies remark, that after having worked a long time upon a ground of black, their eyes were so pained and weakened, they could hardly see. It may perhaps be objected to this theory of the mechanical effect of darkness, that the ill effects of darkness or blackness seem rather mental than corporeal: and I own it is true that they do so; and so do all those that depend on the affections of the finer parts of our system. The ill effects of bad weather appear often no otherwise than in a melancholy and dejection of spirits; though without doubt, in this case, the bodily organs suffer first, and the mind through these organs.

Section 17

THE EFFECTS OF BLACKNESS

Blackness is but a *partial darkness*; and therefore it derives some of its powers from being mixed and surrounded with colored bodies. In its own nature, it cannot be considered as a color. Black bodies, reflecting none, or but a few rays, with regard to sight, are but as so many vacant spaces, dispersed among the objects we view. When the eye lights on one of these vacuities, after having been kept in some degree of tension by the play of the adjacent colors upon it, it suddenly falls into a relaxation; out of which it as suddenly recovers by a convulsive spring. To illustrate this: let us consider that when we intend to sit on a chair, and find it much lower than was expected, the shock is very violent; much more violent than could be thought from so slight a fall as the difference between one chair and another can possibly make. If, after descending a flight of stairs, we attempt inadvertently to take another step in the manner of the former ones, the shock is extremely rude and disagreeable: and by no art can we cause such a shock by the same means when we expect and prepare for it. When I say that this is owing to having the change made contrary to expectation; I do not mean solely, when the *mind* expects. I mean likewise, that when any organ of sense is for some time affected in some one manner, if it suddenly affected otherwise, there ensues a convulsive motion; such a convulsion as is caused when anything happens against the expectance of the mind. And though it may appear strange that such a change as produces a relaxation should immediately produce a sudden convulsion; it is yet most certainly so, and so in all the senses. Every one knows that sleep is a relaxation; and that silence, where nothing keeps the organs of hearing in action, is in general fittest to bring on this relaxation; yet when a sort of murmuring sounds dispose a man to sleep, let these sounds cease suddenly, and the person immediately awakes; that is, the parts are braced up suddenly, and he awakes. This I have often experienced myself, and I have heard the same from observing persons. In like manner, if a person in broad daylight were falling asleep, to introduce a sudden darkness would prevent his sleep for that time, though silence and darkness in themselves, and not suddenly introduced, are very favorable to it. This I knew only by conjecture on the analogy of the senses when I first digested these observations; but I have since experienced it. And I have often experienced, and so have a thousand others, that on the first inclining towards sleep, we have been suddenly awakened with a most violent start; and that this start was generally preceded by a sort of dream of our falling down a precipice: whence does this strange motion arise, but from the too sudden relaxation of the body, which by some mechanism in nature restores itself by as quick and vigorous an exertion of the contracting power of the muscles? The dream itself is caused by this relaxation; and it is of too uniform a nature to be attributed to any other cause. The parts relax too suddenly, which is in the nature of falling; and this accident of the body induces this image in the mind. When we are in a confirmed state of health and vigor, as all changes are then less sudden, and less on the extreme, we can seldom complain of this disagreeable sensation.

Section 18

The Effects of Blackness Moderated

Though the effects of black be painful originally, we must not think they always continue so. Custom reconciles us to everything. After we have been used to the sight of black objects, the terror abates, and the smoothness and glossiness, or some agreeable accident of bodies so colored, softens in some measure the horror and sternness of their original nature; yet the nature of the original impression still continues. Black will always have something melancholy in it, because the sensory will always find the change to it from other colors too violent; or if it occupy the whole compass of the sight, it will then be darkness; and what was said of darkness will be applicable here. I do not purpose to go into all that might be said to illustrate this theory of the effects of light and darkness; neither will I examine all the different effects produced by the various modifications and mixtures of these two causes. If the foregoing observations have any foundation in nature, I conceive them very sufficient to account for all the phenomena that can arise from all the combinations of black with other colors. To enter into every particular, or to answer every objection, would be an endless labor. We have only followed the most leading roads; and we shall observe the same conduct in our inquiry into the cause of beauty.

Section 19

The Physical Cause of Love

When we have before us such objects as excite love and complacency, the body is affected, so far as I could observe, much in the following manner: the head reclines something on one side; the eyelids are more closed than usual, and the eyes roll gently with an inclination to the object; the mouth is a little opened, and the breath drawn slowly, with now and then a low sigh; the whole body is composed, and the hands fall idly to the sides. All this is accompanied with an inward sense of melting and languor. These appearances are always proportioned to the degree of beauty in the object, and of sensibility in the observer. And this gradation from the highest pitch of beauty and sensibility, even to the lowest of mediocrity and indifference, and their correspondent effects, ought to be kept in view, else this description will seem exaggerated, which it certainly is not. But from this description it is almost impossible not to conclude that beauty acts by relaxing the solids of the whole system. There are all the appearances of such a relaxation; and a relaxation somewhat below the natural tone seems to me to be the cause of all positive pleasure. Who is a stranger to that manner of expression so common in all times and in all countries, of being softened, relaxed, enervated, dissolved, melted away by pleasure? The universal voice of mankind, faithful to their feelings, concurs in affirming this uniform and general effect: and although some odd and particular instance may perhaps be found, wherein there appears a considerable degree of positive pleasure, without all the characters of relaxation, we must not therefore reject the conclusion we had drawn from a concurrence of many experiments; but we must still retain it, subjoining the exceptions which may occur according to the judicious rule laid down by Sir Isaac Newton in the third book of his Optics. Our position will, I conceive, appear confirmed beyond any reasonable doubt, if we can show that such things as we have already observed to be the genuine constituents of beauty have each of them, separately taken, a natural tendency to relax the fibres. And if it must be allowed us, that the appearance of the human body, when all these constituents are united together before the sensory, further favors this opinion, we may

　　　　　　　　　　　　　　　　　　EDMUND BURKE

venture, I believe, to conclude that the passion called love is produced by this relaxation. By the same method of reasoning which we have used in the inquiry into the causes of the sublime, we may likewise conclude, that as a beautiful object presented to the sense, by causing a relaxation of the body, produces the passion of love in the mind; so if by any means the passion should first have its origin in the mind, a relaxation of the outward organs will as certainly ensue in a degree proportioned to the cause.

Section 20

Why Smoothness is Beautiful

It is to explain the true cause of visual beauty that I call in the assistance of the other senses. If it appears that *smoothness* is a principal cause of pleasure to the touch, taste, smell, and hearing, it will be easily admitted a constituent of visual beauty; especially as we have before shown, that this quality is found almost without exception in all bodies that are by general consent held beautiful. There can be no doubt that bodies which are rough and angular, rouse and vellicate the organs of feeling, causing a sense of pain, which consists in the violent tension or contraction of the muscular fibres. On the contrary, the application of smooth bodies relaxes; gentle stroking with a smooth hand allays violent pains and cramps, and relaxes the suffering parts from their unnatural tension; and it has therefore very often no mean effect in removing swellings and obstructions. The sense of feeling is highly gratified with smooth bodies. A bed smoothly laid, and soft, that is, where the resistance is every way inconsiderable, is a great luxury, disposing to an universal relaxation, and inducing beyond anything else that species of it called sleep.

Section 21

SWEETNESS, ITS NATURE

N or is it only in the touch that smooth bodies cause positive pleasure by relaxation. In the smell and taste, we find all things agreeable to them, and which are commonly called sweet, to be of a smooth nature, and that they all evidently tend to relax their respective sensories. Let us first consider the taste. Since it is most easy to inquire into the property of liquids, and since all things seem to want a fluid vehicle to make them tasted at all, I intend rather to consider the liquid than the solid parts of our food. The vehicles of all tastes are *water* and *oil*. And what determines the taste is some salt, which affects variously according to its nature, or its manner of being combined with other things. Water and oil, simply considered, are capable of giving some pleasure to the taste. Water, when simple, is insipid, inodorous, colorless, and smooth; it is found, when *not cold*, to be a great resolver of spasms, and lubricator of the fibres; this power it probably owes to its smoothness. For as fluidity depends, according to the most general opinion, on the roundness, smoothness, and weak cohesion of the component parts of any body, and as water acts merely as a simple fluid, it follows that the cause of its fluidity is likewise the cause of its relaxing quality, namely, the smoothness and slippery texture of its parts. The other fluid vehicle of tastes is *oil*. This too, when simple, is insipid, inodorous, colorless, and smooth to the touch and taste. It is smoother than water, and in many cases yet more relaxing. Oil is in some degree pleasant to the eye, the touch, and the taste, insipid as it is. Water is not so grateful; which I do not know on what principle to account for, other than that water is not so soft and smooth. Suppose that to this oil or water were added a certain quantity of a specific salt, which had a power of putting the nervous papillæ of the tongue into a gentle vibratory motion; as suppose sugar dissolved in it. The smoothness of the oil and the vibratory power of the salt cause the sense we call sweetness. In all sweet bodies, sugar, or a substance very little different from sugar, is constantly found. Every species of salt, examined by the microscope, has its own distinct, regular, invariable form. That of nitre is a pointed oblong; that of sea-salt an exact cube; that of sugar a perfect globe. If you have tried how smooth globular bodies, as the marbles with which boys amuse themselves, have affected the touch when they are rolled backward and forward and over one another, you will easily conceive how sweetness, which consists in a salt of such nature, affects the taste; for a single globe (though somewhat pleasant to the feeling), yet by the regularity of its form, and the somewhat too sudden deviation of its parts from a right line, is nothing near so pleasant to the touch as several globes, where the hand gently rises to one and falls to another; and this pleasure is greatly increased if the globes are in motion, and sliding over one another; for this soft variety prevents that weariness, which the uniform disposition of the several globes would otherwise produce. Thus in sweet liquors, the parts of the fluid vehicle, though most probably round, are yet so minute, as to conceal the figure of their component parts from the nicest inquisition of the microscope; and consequently, being so excessively minute, they have a sort of flat simplicity to the taste, resembling the effects of plain smooth bodies to the touch; for if a body be composed of round parts excessively small, and packed pretty closely together, the surface will be both to the sight and touch as if it were nearly plain and smooth. It is clear from their unveiling their figure to the microscope, that the particles of sugar are considerably larger than those of water or oil, and consequently that their effects from their roundness will be more distinct and palpable to the nervous papillæ of that nice organ the tongue; they will induce that sense called sweetness, which in a weak manner we discover in oil, and in a yet weaker in water; for, insipid as they are, water and oil are in some degree sweet; and it may be observed, that insipid things of all kinds approach more nearly to the nature of sweetness than to that of any other taste.

Section 22

Sweetness Relaxing

I n the other senses we have remarked, that smooth things are relaxing. Now it ought to appear that sweet things, which are the smooth of taste, are relaxing too. It is remarkable, that in some languages soft and sweet have but one name. *Doux* in French signifies soft as well as sweet. The Latin *dulcis*, and the Italian *dolce*, have in many cases the same double signification. That sweet things are generally relaxing, is evident; because all such, especially those which are most oily, taken frequently, or in a large quantity, very much enfeeble the tone of the stomach. Sweet smells, which bear a great affinity to sweet tastes, relax very remarkably. The smell of flowers disposes people to drowsiness; and this relaxing effect is further apparent from the prejudice which people of weak nerves receive from their use. It were worth while to examine, whether tastes of this kind, sweet ones, tastes that are caused by smooth oils and a relaxing salt, are not the originally pleasant tastes. For many, which use has rendered such, were not at all agreeable at first. The way to examine this is, to try what nature has originally provided for us, which she has undoubtedly made originally pleasant; and to analyze this provision. *Milk* is the first support of our childhood. The component parts of this are water, oil, and a sort of a very sweet salt, called the sugar of milk. All these when blended have a great *smoothness* to the taste, and a relaxing quality to the skin. The next thing children covet is *fruit*, and of fruits those principally which are sweet; and every one knows that the sweetness of fruit is caused by a subtle oil, and such a salt as that mentioned in the last section. Afterwards custom, habit, the desire of novelty, and a thousand other causes, confound, adulterate, and change our palates, so that we can no longer reason with any satisfaction about them. Before we quit this article, we must observe, that as smooth things are, as such, agreeable to the taste, and are found of a relaxing quality; so on the other hand, things which are found by experience to be of a strengthening quality, and fit to brace the fibres, are almost universally rough and pungent to the taste, and in many cases rough even to the touch. We often apply the quality of sweetness, metaphorically, to visual objects. For the better carrying on this remarkable analogy of the senses, we may here call sweetness the beautiful of the taste.

Section 23

Variation, Why Beautiful

Another principal property of beautiful objects is, that the line of their parts is continually varying its direction; but it varies it by a very insensible deviation; it never varies it so quickly as to surprise, or by the sharpness of its angle to cause any twitching or convulsion of the optic nerve. Nothing long continued in the same manner, nothing very suddenly varied, can be beautiful; because both are opposite to that agreeable relaxation which is the characteristic effect of beauty. It is thus in all the senses. A motion in a right line is that manner of moving, next to a very gentle descent, in which we meet the least resistance; yet it is not that manner of moving, which next to a descent, wearies us the least. Rest certainly tends to relax: yet there is a species of motion which relaxes more than rest; a gentle oscillatory motion, a rising and falling. Rocking sets children to sleep better than absolute rest; there is indeed scarcely anything at that age, which gives more pleasure than to be gently lifted up and down; the manner of playing which their nurses use with children, and the weighing and swinging used afterwards by themselves as a favorite amusement, evince this very sufficiently. Most people must have observed the sort of sense they have had on being swiftly drawn in an easy coach on a smooth turf, with gradual ascents and declivities. This will give a better idea of the beautiful, and point out its probable cause better, than almost anything else. On the contrary, when one is hurried over a rough, rocky, broken road, the pain felt by these sudden inequalities shows why similar sights, feelings, and sounds, are so contrary to beauty: and with regard to the feeling, it is exactly the same in its effect, or very nearly the same, whether, for instance, I move my hand along the surface of a body of a certain shape, or whether such a body is moved along my hand. But to bring this analogy of the senses home to the eye; if a body presented to that sense has such a waving surface, that the rays of light reflected from it are in a continual insensible deviation from the strongest to the weakest (which is always the case in a surface gradually unequal), it must be exactly similar in its effects on the eye and touch; upon the one of which it operates directly, on the other indirectly. And this body will be beautiful if the lines which compose its surface are not continued, even so varied, in a manner that may weary or dissipate the attention. The variation itself must be continually varied.

Section 24

Concerning Smallness

To avoid a sameness which may arise from the too frequent repetition of the same reasonings, and of illustrations of the same nature, I will not enter very minutely into every particular that regards beauty, as it is founded on the disposition of its quantity, or its quantity itself. In speaking of the magnitude of bodies there is great uncertainty, because the ideas of great and small are terms almost entirely relative to the species of the objects, which are infinite. It is true, that having once fixed the species of any object, and the dimensions common in the individuals of that species, we may observe some that exceed, and some that fall short of, the ordinary standard: those which greatly exceed are, by that excess, provided the species itself be not very small, rather great and terrible than beautiful; but as in the animal world, and in a good measure in the vegetable world likewise, the qualities that constitute beauty may possibly be united to things of greater dimensions; when they are so united, they constitute a species something different both from the sublime and beautiful, which I have before called *fine*; but this kind, I imagine, has not such a power on the passions, either as vast bodies have which are endued with the correspondent qualities of the sublime; or as the qualities of beauty have when united in a small object. The affection produced by large bodies adorned with the spoils of beauty, is a tension continually relieved; which approaches to the nature of mediocrity. But if I were to say how I find myself affected upon such occasions, I should say that the sublime suffers less by being united to some of the qualities of beauty, than beauty does by being joined to greatness of quantity, or any other properties of the sublime. There is something so overruling in whatever inspires us with awe, in all things which belong ever so remotely to terror, that nothing else can stand in their presence. There lie the qualities of beauty either dead or unoperative; or at most exerted to mollify the rigor and sternness of the terror, which is the natural concomitant of greatness. Besides the extraordinary great in every species, the opposite to this, the dwarfish and diminutive, ought to be considered. Littleness, merely as such, has nothing contrary to the idea of beauty. The humming-bird, both in shape and coloring, yields to none of the winged species, of which it is the least; and perhaps his beauty is enhanced by his smallness. But there are animals, which, when they are extremely small, are rarely (if ever) beautiful. There is a dwarfish size of men and women, which is almost constantly so gross and massive in comparison of their height, that they present us with a very disagreeable image. But should a man be found not above two or three feet high, supposing such a person to have all the parts of his body of a delicacy suitable to such a size, and otherwise endued with the common qualities of other beautiful bodies, I am pretty well convinced that a person of such a stature might be considered as beautiful; might be the object of love; might give us very pleasing ideas on viewing him. The only thing which could possibly interpose to check our pleasure is, that such creatures, however formed, are unusual, and are often therefore considered as something monstrous. The large and gigantic, though very compatible with the sublime, is contrary to the beautiful. It is impossible to suppose a giant the object of love. When we let our imagination loose in romance, the ideas we naturally annex to that size are those of tyranny, cruelty, injustice, and everything horrid and abominable. We paint the giant ravaging the country, plundering the innocent traveller, and afterwards gorged with his half-living flesh: such are Polyphemus, Cacus, and others, who make so great a figure in romances and heroic poems. The event we attend to with the greatest satisfaction is their defeat and death. I do not remember, in all that multitude of deaths with which the Iliad is filled, that the fall of any man, remarkable for his great stature and strength, touches us with pity; nor does it appear that the author, so well read in human nature, ever intended it should. It is Simoisius, in the soft bloom of youth, torn from his parents, who tremble for a courage so ill suited to his strength; it is another hurried by war from the new embraces of his bride, young and fair, and a novice to the field, who melts us by his untimely fate. Achilles, in spite of the many qualities of beauty which Homer has bestowed on his outward form, and the many great virtues with which he has adorned his mind, can never make us love him. It may be observed, that Homer has given the Trojans, whose fate he has designed to excite our compassion, infinitely more of the amiable, social virtues than he has distributed among his Greeks. With regard to the Trojans, the passion he chooses to raise is pity; pity is a passion founded on love; and these *lesser*, and if I may say domestic virtues, are certainly the most amiable. But he has made the Greeks far their superiors in the politic and military virtues. The councils of Priam are weak; the arms of Hector comparatively feeble; his courage far below that of Achilles. Yet we love Priam more than Agamemnon, and Hector more than his conqueror Achilles. Admiration is the passion which Homer would excite in favor of the Greeks, and he has done it by bestowing on them the virtues which have but little to do with love. This short digression is perhaps not wholly beside our purpose, where our business is to show that objects of great dimensions are incompatible with beauty, the more incompatible as they are greater; whereas the small, if ever they fail of beauty, this failure is not to be attributed to their size.

Section 25

Of Color

With regard to color, the disquisition is almost infinite; but I conceive the principles laid down in the beginning of this part are sufficient to account for the effects of them all, as well as for the agreeable effects of transparent bodies, whether fluid or solid. Suppose I look at a bottle of muddy liquor, of a blue or red color; the blue or red rays cannot pass clearly to the eye, but are suddenly and unequally stopped by the intervention of little opaque bodies, which without preparation change the idea, and change it too into one disagreeable in its own nature, conformably to the principles laid down in Sect. 24. But when the ray passes without such opposition through the glass or liquor, when the glass or liquor is quite transparent, the light is sometimes softened in the passage, which makes it more agreeable even as light; and the liquor reflecting all the rays of its proper color *evenly*, it has such an effect on the eye, as smooth opaque bodies have on the eye and touch. So that the pleasure here is compounded of the softness of the transmitted, and the evenness of the reflected light. This pleasure may be heightened by the common principles in other things, if the shape of the glass which holds the transparent liquor be so judiciously varied, as to present the color gradually and interchangeably, weakened and strengthened with all the variety which judgment in affairs of this nature shall suggest. On a review of all that has been said of the effects, as well as the causes of both, it will appear that the sublime and beautiful are built on principles very different, and that their affections are as different: the great has terror for its basis, which, when it is modified, causes that emotion in the mind, which I have called astonishment; the beautiful is founded on mere positive pleasure, and excites in the soul that feeling which is called love. Their causes have made the subject of this fourth part.

PART 5

Section 1

Of Words

Natural objects affect us by the laws of that connection which Providence has established between certain motions and configurations of bodies, and certain consequent feelings in our mind. Painting affects in the same manner, but with the superadded pleasure of imitation. Architecture affects by the laws of nature and the law of reason; from which latter result the rules of proportion, which make a work to be praised or censured, in the whole or in some part, when the end for which it was designed is or is not properly answered. But as to words; they seem to me to affect us in a manner very different from that in which we are affected by natural objects, or by painting or architecture; yet words have as considerable a share in exciting ideas of beauty and of the sublime as many of those, and sometimes a much greater than any of them; therefore an inquiry into the manner by which they excite such emotions is far from being unnecessary in a discourse of this kind.

Section 2

The Common Effects of Poetry, Not By Raising Ideas of Things

The common notion of the power of poetry and eloquence, as well as that of words in ordinary conversation, is, that they affect the mind by raising in it ideas of those things for which custom has appointed them to stand. To examine the truth of this notion, it may be requisite to observe that words may be divided into three sorts. The first are such as represent many simple ideas *united by nature* to form some one determinate composition, as man, horse, tree, castle, &c. These I call *aggregate words*. The second are they that stand for one simple idea of such compositions, and no more; as red, blue, round, square, and the like. These I call *simple abstract* words. The third are those which are formed by an union, an *arbitrary* union of both the others, and of the various relations between them in greater or lesser degrees of complexity; as virtue, honor, persuasion, magistrate, and the like. These I call *compound abstract* words. Words, I am sensible, are capable of being classed into more curious distinctions; but these seem to be natural, and enough for our purpose; and they are disposed in that order in which they are commonly taught, and in which the mind gets the ideas they are substituted for. I shall begin with the third sort of words; compound abstracts, such as virtue, honor, persuasion, docility. Of these I am convinced, that whatever power they may have on the passions, they do not derive it from any representation raised in the mind of the things for which they stand. As compositions, they are not real essences, and hardly cause, I think, any real ideas. Nobody, I believe, immediately on hearing the sounds, virtue, liberty, or honor, conceives any precise notions of the particular modes of action and thinking, together with the mixed and simple ideas, and the several relations of them for which these words are substituted; neither has he any general idea compounded of them; for if he had, then some of those particular ones, though indistinct perhaps, and confused, might come soon to be perceived. But this, I take it, is hardly ever the case. For, put yourself upon analyzing one of these words, and you must reduce it from one set of general words to another, and then into the simple abstracts and aggregates, in a much longer series than may be at first imagined, before any real idea emerges to light, before you come to discover anything like the first principles of such compositions; and when you have made such a discovery of the original ideas, the effect of the composition is utterly lost. A train of thinking of this sort is much too long to be pursued in the ordinary ways of conversation; nor is it at all necessary that it should. Such words are in reality but mere sounds; but they are sounds which being used on particular occasions, wherein we receive some good, or suffer some evil; or see others affected with good or evil; or which we hear applied to other interesting things or events; and being applied in such a variety of cases, that we know readily by habit to what things they belong, they produce in the mind, whenever they are afterwards mentioned, effects similar to those of their occasions. The sounds being often used without reference to any particular occasion, and carrying still their first impressions, they at last utterly lose their connection with the particular occasions that gave rise to them; yet the sound, without any annexed notion, continues to operate as before.

Section 3

General Words Before Ideas

M r. Locke has somewhere observed, with his usual sagacity, that most general words, those belonging to virtue and vice, good and evil especially, are taught before the particular modes of action to which they belong are presented to the mind; and with them, the love of the one, and the abhorrence of the other; for the minds of children are so ductile, that a nurse, or any person about a child, by seeming pleased or displeased with anything, or even any word, may give the disposition of the child a similar turn. When, afterwards, the several occurrences in life come to be applied to these words, and that which is pleasant often appears under the name of evil; and what is disagreeable to nature is called good and virtuous; a strange confusion of ideas and affections arises in the minds of many; and an appearance of no small contradiction between their notions and their actions. There are many who love virtue and who detest vice, and this not from hypocrisy or affectation, who notwithstanding very frequently act ill and wickedly in particulars without the least remorse; because these particular occasions never came into view, when the passions on the side of virtue were so warmly affected by certain words heated originally by the breath of others; and for this reason, it is hard to repeat certain sets of words, though owned by themselves unoperative, without being in some degree affected; especially if a warm and affecting tone of voice accompanies them, as suppose,

Wise, valiant, generous, good, and great.

These words, by having no application, ought to be unoperative; but when words commonly sacred to great occasions are used, we are affected by them even without the occasions. When words which have been generally so applied are put together without any rational view, or in such a manner that they do not rightly agree with each other, the style is called bombast. And it requires in several cases much good sense and experience to be guarded against the force of such language; for when propriety is neglected, a greater number of these affecting words may be taken into the service, and a greater variety may be indulged in combining them.

Section 4

THE EFFECT OF WORDS

If words have all their possible extent of power, three effects arise
in the mind of the hearer. The first is, the *sound*; the second, the
picture, or representation of the thing signified by the sound; the third
is, the *affection* of the soul produced by one or by both of the foregoing.
Compounded abstract words, of which we have been speaking, (honor,
justice, liberty, and the like,) produce the first and the last of these effects,
but not the second. *Simple abstracts* are used to signify some one simple
idea without much adverting to others which may chance to attend it, as
blue, green, hot, cold, and the like; these are capable of affecting all three
of the purposes of words; as the *aggregate* words, man, castle, horse, &c.
are in a yet higher degree. But I am of opinion, that the most general
effect, even of these words, does not arise from their forming pictures
of the several things they would represent in the imagination; because,
on a very diligent examination of my own mind, and getting others to
consider theirs, I do not find that once in twenty times any such picture
is formed, and when it is, there is most commonly a particular effort of
the imagination for that purpose. But the aggregate words operate, as
I said of the compound-abstracts, not by presenting any image to the
mind, but by having from use the same effect on being mentioned, that
their original has when it is seen. Suppose we were to read a passage
to this effect: "The river Danube rises in a moist and mountainous soil
in the heart of Germany, where, winding to and fro, it waters several
principalities, until, turning into Austria, and laving the walls of
Vienna, it passes into Hungary; there with a vast flood, augmented by
the Save and the Drave, it quits Christendom, and rolling through the
barbarous countries which border on Tartary, it enters by many mouths
in the Black Sea." In this description many things are mentioned, as
mountains, rivers, cities, the sea, &c. But let anybody examine himself,
and see whether he has had impressed on his imagination any pictures
of a river, mountain, watery soil, Germany, &c. Indeed it is impossible,
in the rapidity and quick succession of words in conversation, to have
ideas both of the sound of the word, and of the thing represented;
besides, some words, expressing real essences, are so mixed with others

of a general and nominal import, that it is impracticable to jump from sense to thought, from particulars to generals, from things to words, in such a manner as to answer the purposes of life; nor is it necessary that we should.

Section 5

EXAMPLES THAT WORDS MAY AFFECT
WITHOUT RAISING IMAGES

I find it very hard to persuade several that their passions are affected by words from whence they have no ideas; and yet harder to convince them that in the ordinary course of conversation we are sufficiently understood without raising any images of the things concerning which we speak. It seems to be an odd subject of dispute with any man, whether he has ideas in his mind or not. Of this, at first view, every man, in his own forum, ought to judge without appeal. But, strange as it may appear, we are often at a loss to know what ideas we have of things, or whether we have any ideas at all upon some subjects. It even requires a good deal of attention to be thoroughly satisfied on this head. Since I wrote these papers, I found two very striking instances of the possibility there is, that a man may hear words without having any idea of the things which they represent, and yet afterwards be capable of returning them to others, combined in a new way, and with great propriety, energy, and instruction. The first instance is that of Mr. Blacklock, a poet blind from his birth. Few men blessed with the most perfect sight can describe visual objects with more spirit and justness than this blind man; which cannot possibly be attributed to his having a clearer conception of the things he describes than is common to other persons. Mr. Spence, in an elegant preface which he has written to the works of this poet, reasons very ingeniously, and, I imagine, for the most part, very rightly, upon the cause of this extraordinary phenomenon; but I cannot altogether agree with him, that some improprieties in language and thought, which occur in these poems, have arisen from the blind poet's imperfect conception of visual objects, since such improprieties, and much greater, may be found in writers even of a higher class than Mr. Blacklock, and who, notwithstanding, possessed the faculty of seeing in its full perfection. Here is a poet doubtless as much affected by his own descriptions as any that reads them can be; and yet he is affected with this strong enthusiasm by things of which he neither has, nor can possibly have, any idea further than that of a bare sound: and why may not those who read his works be affected in the same manner that he was; with as little of any real ideas of the things described? The second instance is of Mr. Saunderson, professor of mathematics in the University of Cambridge. This learned man had acquired great knowledge in natural philosophy, in astronomy, and whatever sciences depend upon mathematical skill. What was the most extraordinary and the most to my purpose, he gave excellent lectures upon light and colors; and this man taught others the theory of those ideas which they had, and which he himself undoubtedly had not. But it is probable that the words red, blue, green, answered to him as well as the ideas of the colors themselves; for the ideas of greater or lesser degrees of refrangibility being applied to these words, and the blind man being instructed in what other respects they were found to agree or to disagree, it was as easy for him to reason upon the words as if he had been fully master of the ideas. Indeed it must be owned he could make no new discoveries in the way of experiment. He did nothing but what we do every day in common discourse. When I wrote this last sentence, and used the words *every day* and *common discourse*, I had no images in my mind of any succession of time; nor of men in conference with each other; nor do I imagine that the reader will have any such ideas on reading it. Neither when I spoke of red, or blue, and green, as well as refrangibility, had I these several colors, or the rays of light passing into a different medium, and there diverted from their course, painted before me in the way of images. I know very well that the mind possesses a faculty of raising such images at pleasure; but then an act of the will is necessary to this; and in ordinary conversation or reading it is very rarely that any image at all is excited in the mind. If I say, "I shall go to Italy next summer," I am well understood. Yet I believe nobody has by this painted in his imagination the exact figure of the speaker passing by land or by water, or both; sometimes on horseback, sometimes in a carriage: with all the particulars of the journey. Still less has he any idea of Italy, the country to which I proposed to go; or of the greenness of the fields, the ripening of the fruits, and the warmth of the air, with the change to this from a different season, which are the ideas for which the word *summer* is substituted; but least of all has he any image from the word *next*; for this word stands for the idea of many summers, with the exclusion of all but one: and surely the man who says *next summer* has no images of such a succession, and such an exclusion. In short, it is not only of those ideas which are commonly called abstract, and of which no image at all can be formed, but even of particular, real beings, that we converse without having any idea of them excited in the imagination; as will certainly appear on a diligent examination of our own minds. Indeed, so little does poetry depend for its effect on the power of raising sensible images, that I am convinced it would lose a very considerable part of its energy, if this were the necessary result of all description. Because that union of affecting words, which is the most powerful of all poetical instruments, would frequently lose its force along with its propriety and consistency, if the sensible images were always excited. There is not, perhaps, in the whole Æneid a more grand and labored passage than the description of Vulcan's cavern in Etna, and the works that are there carried on. Virgil dwells particularly on the formation of the thunder which he describes unfinished under the hammers of the Cyclops. But what are the principles of this extraordinary composition?

Tres imbris torti radios, tres nubis aquosæ
Addiderant; rutili tres ignis, et alitis austri:
Fulgores nunc terrificos, sonitumque, metumque
Miscebant operi, flammisque sequacibus iras.

This seems to me admirably sublime: yet if we attend coolly to the kind of sensible images which a combination of ideas of this sort must form, the chimeras of madmen cannot appear more wild and absurd than such a picture. "*Three rays of twisted showers, three of watery clouds, three of fire, and three of the winged south wind; then mixed they in the work terrific lightnings, and sound, and fear, and anger, with pursuing flames.*" This strange composition is formed into a gross body; it is hammered by the Cyclops, it is in part polished, and partly continues rough. The truth is, if poetry gives us a noble assemblage of words corresponding to many noble ideas, which are connected by circumstances of time or place, or related to each other as cause and effect, or associated in any natural way, they may be moulded together in any form, and perfectly answer their end. The picturesque connection is not demanded; because no real picture is formed; nor is the effect of the description at all the less upon this account. What is said of Helen by Priam and the old men of his council, is generally thought to give us the highest possible idea of that fatal beauty.

"*They cried, No wonder such celestial charms*
For nine long years have set the world in arms;

What winning graces! what majestic mien!
She moves a goddess, and she looks a queen."

—P<small>OPE</small>

Here is not one word said of the particulars of her beauty; nothing which can in the least help us to any precise idea of her person; but yet we are much more touched by this manner of mentioning her, than by those long and labored descriptions of Helen, whether handed down by tradition, or formed by fancy, which are to be met with in some authors. I am sure it affects me much more than the minute description which Spenser has given of Belphebe; though I own that there are parts, in that description, as there are in all the descriptions of that excellent writer, extremely fine and poetical. The terrible picture which Lucretius has drawn of religion in order to display the magnanimity of his philosophical hero in opposing her, is thought to be designed with great boldness and spirit:—

Humana ante oculos foedè cum vita jaceret,
In terris, oppressa gravi sub religione,
Quæ caput e coeli regionibus ostendebat
Horribili super aspectu mortalibus instans;
Primus Graius homo mortales tollere contra
Est oculos ausus.

What idea do you derive from so excellent a picture? none at all, most certainly: neither has the poet said a single word which might in the least serve to mark a single limb or feature of the phantom, which he intended to represent in all the horrors imagination can conceive. In reality, poetry and rhetoric do not succeed in exact description so well as painting does; their business is, to affect rather by sympathy than imitation; to display rather the effect of things on the mind of the speaker, or of others, than to present a clear idea of the things themselves. This is their most extensive province, and that in which they succeed the best.

Section 6

POETRY NOT STRICTLY AN IMITATIVE ART

Hence we may observe that poetry, taken in its most general sense, cannot with strict propriety be called an art of imitation. It is indeed an imitation so far as it describes the manners and passions of men which their words can express; where *animi motus effert interprete lingua*. There it is strictly imitation; and all merely *dramatic* poetry is of this sort. But *descriptive* poetry operates chiefly by *substitution*; by the means of sounds, which by custom have the effect of realities. Nothing is an imitation further than as it resembles some other thing; and words undoubtedly have no sort of resemblance to the ideas for which they stand.

Section 7

How Words Influence the Passions

Now, as words affect, not by any original power, but by representation, it might be supposed, that their influence over the passions should be but light; yet it is quite otherwise; for we find by experience, that eloquence and poetry are as capable, nay indeed much more capable, of making deep and lively impressions than any other arts, and even than nature itself in very many cases. And this arises chiefly from these three causes. First, that we take an extraordinary part in the passions of others, and that we are easily affected and brought into sympathy by any tokens which are shown of them; and there are no tokens which can express all the circumstances of most passions so fully as words; so that if a person speaks upon any subject, he can not only convey the subject to you, but likewise the manner in which he is himself affected by it. Certain it is, that the influence of most things on our passions is not so much from the things themselves, as from our opinions concerning them; and these again depend very much on the opinions of other men, conveyable for the most part by words only. Secondly, there are many things of a very affecting nature, which can seldom occur in the reality, but the words that represent them often do; and thus they have an opportunity of making a deep impression and taking root in the mind, whilst the idea of the reality was transient; and to some perhaps never really occurred in any shape, to whom it is notwithstanding very affecting, as war, death, famine, &c. Besides many ideas have never been at all presented to the senses of any men but by words, as God, angels, devils, heaven, and hell, all of which have however a great influence over the passions. Thirdly, by words we have it in our power to make such *combinations* as we cannot possibly do otherwise. By this power of combining we are able, by the addition of well-chosen circumstances, to give a new life and force to the simple object. In painting we may represent any fine figure we please; but we never can give it those enlivening touches which it may receive from words. To represent an angel in a picture, you can only draw a beautiful young man winged: but what painting can furnish out anything so grand as the addition of one word, "the angel of the *Lord*"? It is true, I have here no clear idea; but these words affect the mind more than the sensible image did; which is all I contend for. A picture of Priam dragged to the altar's foot, and there murdered, if it were well executed, would undoubtedly be very moving; but there are very aggravating circumstances, which it could never represent:

Sanguine foedantem quos ipse sacraverat *ignes.*

As a further instance, let us consider those lines of Milton, where he describes the travels of the fallen angels through their dismal habitation:

"O'er many a dark and dreary vale
They passed, and many a region dolorous;
O'er many a frozen, many a fiery Alp;
Rocks, caves, lakes, fens, bogs, dens, and shades of death,
A universe of death."

Here is displayed the force of union in

"Rocks, caves, lakes, dens, bogs, fens, and shades"

which yet would lose the greatest part of their effect, if they were not the

"Rocks, caves, lakes, dens, bogs, fens, and shades—of Death."

This idea or this affection caused by a word, which nothing but a word could annex to the others, raises a very great degree of the sublime, and this sublime is raised yet higher by what follows, a *"universe of death."* Here are again two ideas not presentable but by language, and an union of them great and amazing beyond conception; if they may properly be called ideas which present no distinct image to the mind; but still it will be difficult to conceive how words can move the passions which belong to real objects, without representing these objects clearly. This is difficult to us, because we do not sufficiently distinguish, in our observations upon language, between a clear expression and a strong expression. These are frequently confounded with each other, though they are in reality extremely different. The former regards the understanding, the latter belongs to the passions. The one describes a thing as it is, the latter describes it as it is felt. Now, as there is a moving tone of voice, an impassioned countenance, an agitated gesture, which affect independently of the things about which they are exerted, so there are words, and certain dispositions of words, which being peculiarly devoted to passionate subjects, and always used by those who are under the influence of any passion, touch and move us more than those which far more clearly and distinctly express the subject-matter. We yield to sympathy what we refuse to description. The truth is, all verbal description, merely as naked description, though never so exact, conveys so poor and insufficient an idea of the thing described, that it could scarcely have the smallest effect, if the speaker did not call in to his aid those modes of speech that mark a strong and lively feeling in himself. Then, by the contagion of our passions, we catch a fire already kindled in another, which probably might never have been struck out by the object described. Words, by strongly conveying the passions by those means which we have already mentioned, fully compensate for their weakness in other respects. It may be observed, that very polished languages, and such as are praised for their superior clearness and perspicuity, are generally deficient in strength. The French language has that perfection and that defect. Whereas the Oriental tongues, and in general the languages of most unpolished people, have a great force and energy of expression, and this is but natural. Uncultivated people are but ordinary observers of things, and not critical in distinguishing them; but, for that reason they admire more, and are more affected with what they see, and therefore express themselves in a warmer and more passionate manner. If the affection be well conveyed, it will work its effect without any clear idea, often without any idea at all of the thing which has originally given rise to it.

It might be expected, from the fertility of the subject, that I should consider poetry, as it regards the sublime and beautiful, more at large; but it must be observed, that in this light it has been often and well handled already. It was not my design to enter into the criticism of the sublime and beautiful in any art, but to attempt to lay down such principles as may tend to ascertain, to distinguish, and to form a sort of standard for them; which purposes I thought might be best effected by an inquiry into the properties of such things in nature, as raise love and astonishment in us; and by showing in what manner they operated to produce these passions. Words were only so far to be considered as to show upon what principle they were capable of being the representatives of these natural things, and by what powers they were able to affect us often as strongly as the things they represent, and sometimes much more strongly.

EDMUND BURKE

A Note About the Author

Edmund Burke (1729–1797) was an Irish philosopher and member of parliament in the British House of Commons. The son of a Catholic mother and Anglican father, Burke was raised between Dublin and rural County Cork. In 1744, he began studying at Trinity College Dublin, where he founded a debating society and graduated in 1748. Burke traveled to London in 1750 to become a lawyer, but soon abandoned his legal studies in favor of a life of professional writing. His first work, *A Vindication of Natural Society: A View of the Miseries and Evils Arising to Mankind* (1756) was an ironic reworking of Lord Bolingbroke's infamous arguments for reason over religion. This satire earned Burke the reputation of fearless firebrand and intellectual skeptic which would carry him throughout his career. His two most important publications, arguably, are *A Philosophical Enquiry into the Origin of Our Ideas of the Sublime and Beautiful* (1757) and *Reflections on the Revolution in France* (1790). Although a member of the historically liberal Whig Party, Burke is now frequently seen as a foundational figure in the development of modern conservative thought.

A Note from the Publisher

Spanning many genres, from non-fiction essays to literature classics to children's books and lyric poetry, Mint Edition books showcase the master works of our time in a modern new package. The text is freshly typeset, is clean and easy to read, and features a new note about the author in each volume. Many books also include exclusive new introductory material. Every book boasts a striking new cover, which makes it as appropriate for collecting as it is for gift giving. Mint Edition books are only printed when a reader orders them, so natural resources are not wasted. We're proud that our books are never manufactured in excess and exist only in the exact quantity they need to be read and enjoyed.

bookfinity™

Discover more of your favorite classics with Bookfinity™.

- Track your reading with custom book lists.
- Get great book recommendations for your personalized Reader Type.
- Add reviews for your favorite books.
- AND MUCH MORE!

Visit **bookfinity.com** and take the fun Reader Type quiz to get started.

Enjoy our classic and modern companion pairings!

Printed in the USA
CPSIA information can be obtained
at www.ICGtesting.com
JSHW082338140824
68134JS00020B/1743